inscribed

For Joy

with warm best wishes
for the future

[signature]

FAITH — FAMILY — FRIENDS

Previous Books by Thomas Patrick Melady

Profiles of African Leaders
White Man's Future in Africa
Faces of Africa
Kenneth Kaunda of Zambia
Revolution of Color
Western Policy and the Third World
House Divided
Development: Lessons for the Future (Co-author)
Burundi: The Tragic Years
Uganda: The Asian Exiles
Idi Amin: Hitler in Africa (Co-author)
The Ambassador's Story
Catholics in the Public Square (Editor)
Public Catholicism (Editor)
Witness to the Faith (Editor)

FAITH — FAMILY — FRIENDS

A Few Glances
at the Life of
Thomas Patrick Melady
Diplomat – Educator – Soldier

Copyright © 2003 by Thomas Patrick Melady

ALL RIGHTS RESERVED
Rutledge Books, Inc.

Manufactured in the United States of America

Cataloging in Publication Data
Melady, Thomas Patrick
    Faith, Family, Friends

    ISBN: 1-58244-263-0

        1. Memoir   3. Uganda
        2. Burundi   4. Vatican-U.S. relations

Library of Congress Control Number: 2003102112

To My Wife Margaret
My Daughters Christina and Monica
and Grandchildren
Alexandra
Nicolas
Samantha
Zachary
and the next arrival

ACKNOWLEDGMENTS

Toni Mendez, my literary agent, urged me to write a memoir about twelve important periods in my life. She advised me after reading the first draft and I am grateful to her for the counsel on this book as with my previous ones.

My work on this very personal project took place in Washington and Rome. Todd Calongne, Igor Raznatovic and Ricardo Pachon Chaves assisted me with the preparation.

Once completed, John Wobensmith read the entire manuscript and gave me some valuable advice. The same with John Lenczowski, Director of The Institute of World Politics.

My wife, Margaret who entered my life as I was writing my second book gave encouragement and counsel on this project as with previous ones.

The Institute of World Politics, Washington, D.C., for its cooperation.

Thanks for all your assistance.

Published in cooperation with
The Institute of World Politics,
Washington, D.C.

Table of Contents

Chapter I — High School: Pain and Pleasure   **1**
- Alienation Starts in the Neighborhood   3
- Finding Two Friends: the Two Georges   6
- Pressure Buildup   7
- The Other George   8
- Different Roads: Two Good Men   9
- A Week Later: Into the Army   11

Chapter II — Aunt Emma: Photo Albums and Marigold Flowers   **13**
- High school   15
- The Photo Albums   16
- War   17
- Christmas is Different Now   18
- Into the Army   20

Chapter III — The Army: New Horizons   **23**
- Christmas in Rome   25
- German POW's   26

Visits to Austria, Germany and Switzerland	28
The Black Market	30
Need for Service	31
Thoughts About The Future	32
Focus on the Family Situation	34

Chapter IV — University Studies: At Long Last   **39**

Religious Pluralism	40
The Catholic University of America	43
Conservative or Liberal: Which way?	44
The International Relations Club	46
Father John Courtney Murray: An Inspiration	47
Call to Active Duty; Rumors on Campus	49

Chapter V — Baby Joe, Harvard and the Episcopal Church   **53**

Sent to Ethiopia and Return	55
Harvard and the Episcopal Church	57

Chapter VI — Margaret, African Affairs, and Exciting Times   **61**

Youth Service Abroad: The Peace Corps	62
Three Jobs	64
Margaret	67

Chapter VII — Burundi and Uganda: The Reality of Brutality   **75**

Uganda	83
Expulsion of the Asians	84
Approval of Hitler	86
Return to the U.S.A.	89

Chapter VIII — Presidents Nyerere, Nixon and the Maryknoll Sisters — 99

    Appointment with President Nixon — 100
    A Previous Appointment — 101
    Appointment with President Nyerere — 102
    Kenneth Kaunda: Dirty Faces — 105

Chapter IX — St. Joseph's University and Sacred Heart University: Tranquility and Discomfort — 107

    Margaret; Teaching at the University — 109
    A Shadow Over the Eucharistic Congress — 109
    Conference on World Hunger — 110
    Sacred Heart University: A New Challenge — 112
    School Politics — 114
    Experience with Mistreatment of the Marginalized — 117

Chapter X — My Four Happy and Unforgettable Years at the Vatican — 123

    Tell the President What You Want — 123
    Christmas Eve and Noriega — 125
    The State of Israel and the Holy See:
        Complex Relationships — 131
    The Gulf War: No Convergence — 133
    The Convergence's and the Differences — 135
    The Problem: the Fifth and Sixth Criteria — 137
    Not Pacifist at Any Cost — 138
    Ground Offensive — 141
    No Action Against Saddam Hussein — 142
    President Bush Visits the Pope — 144
    Personal Experience — 147
    Time to say good-bye — 169

Chapter XI — The Last Goodbye: Only 10 Minutes   **151**
   Mid October 1950   152
   Final Goodbye   154

**Chapter XII — Memories of Blueberries and
A Kiss On The Lips**   **157**

Biographical Note

Thomas Patrick Melady was born on March 4, 1927 and raised in Norwich, Connecticut. Following his military service and university studies he served in various diplomatic posts, primarily as U.S. Ambassador to Burundi, Uganda and the Vatican, and senior adviser to the U.S. delegation to the U.N. General Assembly.

His career in higher education included serving as Executive Vice President of St. Joseph's University and President of Sacred Heart University. He is also a former Assistant U.S. Secretary of Postsecondary Education. He has served as a Visiting Professor at St. John's University, Seton Hall University, George Washington University and The American University of Rome. Ambassador Melady has also served as a consultant to governments, corporations and universities.

He is the author or editor of fifteen books. Twenty-eight Universities have conferred honorary doctorates on him. Ambassador Melady has also been honored by the Vatican with three awards and by five foreign countries. He received his B.A. degree from Duquesne University and his M.A. and Ph.D. degrees from the Catholic University of America.

He is active with two international organizations, the Sovereign Military Order of Malta where he is a Knight in Obedience, and the Sacred Military Constantinian Order of St. George, where he is the Vice Delegate for the United States. He is now the senior diplomat in residence and Professor at The Institute of World Politics in Washington, D.C. He is married to Margaret J. Badum, President of the American University of Rome. They are the parents of two adult daughters.

Introduction

My youth was spent in the working class quarters of Norwich, a city in eastern Connecticut. I was born into a loving family which had very minimal educational opportunities. Many opportunities however, were made available to me. I had four senior diplomatic appointments and represented my country in challenging, dangerous and interesting assignments.

The modest background did not prevent me from serving in these diplomatic roles nor as a university president and as the chief federal officer for higher education.

In this book I share these experiences with you as well as the lessons I learned about the values of faith, family, friends and commitment.

There are areas where I was proud of my accomplishments but there were other situations where I believe my responses were inadequate. In the several instances where my experiences involved families and friends who are still living, I used other names and altered some of the circumstances to assure privacy.

Some of my experiences were on the world stage and have some historical significance. Other experiences come from cross-cultural contacts, which had some interesting implications. I begin by setting the background of my early youth and end with saying the final goodbye to my mother and to friends of many years.

Thomas P. Melady

CHAPTER 1

HIGH SCHOOL: PAIN AND PLEASURE

I WAS ONE OF TWO MEMBERS OF MY GRADUATING CLASS OF BISHOP School, on the East side of Norwich who applied for the classical studies program at the Norwich Free Academy. This was a private non-denominational secondary school where the city of Norwich provided secondary level education by paying the tuition of Norwich students who enrolled there.

I spent my boyhood in the East Side of Norwich which was one of the town's working class sections. Norwich was an old New England town in the eastern part of Connecticut, north of the port city of New London and near the Rhode Island border.

My Irish grandparents settled in neighboring Jewett City and my French-Canadian grandparents migrated to Taftville, a then French-Canadian enclave in Norwich. They were all employed in textile mills. The East Side of Norwich was mostly Irish, Italian, and Polish, along with a substantial number of working class Protestants. A Jewish community lived on the West Side, the other working class section of Norwich. I was born in Jewett City, but after my father and uncle's small trucking business failed, the family moved to the East Side of Norwich. There, my father found a job as a truck driver with the Thames River Line, which paid him twenty-seven dollars and fifty cents a week. My mother supplemented the family income by renting rooms to tourists. My sisters Peg and Pat and my brother Mark and I lived with our parents, Tom and Rose Belisle Melady, in modest circumstances.

My peers at Bishop School, the local public school where I would spend nine years, came from the same kind of background. It was the 1930s and unemployment was rampant as a result of the Depression. The economic situation improved somewhat with the start of World War II in 1939. When I graduated from high school in 1945 the nation was nearly at full employment. The East Side retained its distinct working class culture. I never forgot my origins, which had an impact on my life.

I was close to the top of my class at Bishop School. This gave me a special confidence. When, in 1941, I applied for admission to the classical studies program at the Norwich Free Academy, I knew then that I wanted one day to attend a university. This was probably the first critical decision in my life.

When a counselor at the Academy interviewed me, I was surprised to be told that the Bishop School did not have a good record of preparing students for either the classical or scientific studies program. Since the student body at Bishop School was overwhelmingly from working class families who were not thinking about college, the level of class instruction was for students going into commercial or trade schools. Nevertheless, I was accepted into the classical studies program of the Academy.

Despite this, I have very good memories of Bishop School. Most of what I knew about the world outside came from my stamp collection, which gave me a few fascinating snapshots of the rest of the world. I made my first excursion outside of Connecticut when my eighth grade class went for a one-day field trip to New York City. My mother gave me one dollar for the day, making quite a dent in our family's weekly budget. Miss Marguerite Foley, Principal and eighth grade teacher, was our chaperon for what was for many of us our first visit to the big city.

I spent nine years at Bishop School starting with the kindergarten. Miss Foley was stern and loved by all as she cared for us. Later in life, while a student in high school, in the Army, or at the University, I would drop in to see her.

The trip to New York was the "thrill of the year" for me. Following graduation from Bishop School, I spent the summer preparing for my studies at the Academy.

The counselor who interviewed me gave me a list of books that I should read before starting my classes at the Academy. I accepted the advice and went to Norwich's Otis Library every Monday to take out the books. I attacked the assignments enthusiastically. After helping my mother with household chores, I would spend the afternoon reading. On Saturday I worked for Aunt Emma or did other jobs.

Alienation Starts in the Neighborhood

It was during the summer of 1941, while completing the reading assignment, that I felt the first signs of alienation from my boyhood friends on the East Side. They did all the things that fourteen-year-old boys from working class families do. I, on the other hand, was reading books. One of my frequent playmates, who lived on the same street, asked me if I thought I was "better than everyone else!"

The local boys gathered around Louie's street corner store. I did not. Sometimes on Monday, when I would return books to the library (usually a good four or five of them), I would be taunted as "quiz kid" as I walked by the street corner. Some of the other names were less complimentary. I was slowly being excluded from my local peer group.

My parents were generally supportive of my goals. My dad had only one regret: I did not play baseball. In fact, I really did not play any sports, although I took up swimming at the YMCA in my second year at the Academy.

I began my studies in September with great enthusiasm. A month later, I experienced the first truly shocking incident in this period of my life.

Two of my teeth became infected and could not be extracted until the swelling subsided. The local East Side dentist only extracted teeth and drilled for fillings. It was an excruciating experience. My mother wrapped a cold towel around my head that I kept on for ten days. Finally, after much pain, the two teeth were extracted. The entire ordeal had lasted two weeks. Not only did I miss my classes, but I was also unable to study because of the pain.

This was a near disaster for my beginning at the Academy. I found myself behind in algebra, Latin, English literature and ancient history. My counselor, Signe Seaberg, summoned me to her office and said, "Tom, you need a tutor to make up for the classes missed." She reminded me that I came ill prepared from Bishop School and was in a precarious academic situation.

She gave me a list of tutors. The charge would be seventy-five cents an hour. I thanked her but never bothered to discuss the matter with my mother as I knew that money was very tight. The next day Ms. Seaberg stopped me in the hallway at school and inquired about my plans. I said that I would stay at the Academy each afternoon and study the chapters that were discussed in the classes I had missed. She seemed distressed and asked me to come to her office after my classes.

When I reported to her after class, she closed the door and asked me about my career plans. I told her that my dream was to attend a university and to become a lawyer. Then, to my surprise, she inquired about my parents. I told her that my dad was a truck driver and that my mother rented rooms to tourists.

Given my background and the inadequate elementary school preparation, she observed that I was "overreaching." Since, as she described, I had studious habits, she proposed that I think about becoming a bookkeeper, a career that would only require a high school diploma in commercial studies. She said that she would authorize my transfer the next day.

I immediately responded by thanking her and saying that I intended to remain in the classical studies program. I never told my parents about the conversation, but that evening I quietly cried myself to sleep. I felt lonely without anyone to consult on these matters. There were quite a few lonely evenings during my high school days.

The next few weeks were tough, especially in algebra and Latin. By the end of the semester, my grades were quite decent—B's with an A in ancient history. I still had little or no time for my neighborhood friends. By Christmas I felt two pains: growing separation from my neighborhood peer group and the realization that I was the product of a loving but a modest cultural background. I wondered how I would do in the competitive college preparatory course. I came to the conclusion that the "walk up the hill" to university studies and a professional life would not be an easy one.

Every afternoon I was at the library and on Saturdays I worked for Aunt Emma. I began to hear the comment "who did I think I was" more and more often. Even several aunts told me that I "studied too much."

Since I no longer played with my friends, I devoted more time to my stamp collecting hobby. One benefit of this pursuit was that I had become familiar with the countries of the world and their capitals. I even won the state "quiz-kid" contest, and with it a twenty-five dollar war savings bond. It was quite a morale booster and I was congratulated by several of my teachers at the Academy.

Finding Two Friends: the Two Georges

We were members of Norwich's St. Mary's Church, which served the East Side and Greenville. I became attached to Father Donahue, the Pastor, and looked forward to his sermons. He would quote extensively from Cardinal Newman. We normally went as a family to the 9 a.m. Mass on Sundays. Afterward, there was Sunday school. My sisters and I would walk home. It was a one and a half-mile hike. When the family car did not work, we walked both ways.

I would drop in to see Father George Donahue and tell him about my insecurities. He gave me the straight Catholic message: go to Mass and Communion every Sunday and make a confession at least once a month. While I had little formal education in Catholic teachings until university, I held on to the Catholic faith from high school onward.

Father Donahue was also an intellectual in an overwhelmingly working class parish. He would encourage me to read certain books, and even gave me a few. I stayed in touch with him throughout my four years at the Academy.

My sophomore year was the roughest. French was added to my course work. I did enjoy swimming at the YMCA, which counted as an elective course. I swam three times a week and became involved in several youth activities, especially the Hi-Y movement of the YMCA. Classes at the Academy started at 8 a.m., which meant that I had to leave the house around seven for the one and three-quarter mile walk. I always had three to five books with me from the previous day and evening of study. My neighborhood friends from the East Side would frequently walk with me not carrying a single book. They sometimes enjoyed taunting me about the library that I carried with me each day.

Pressure Buildup

As I devoted more time to swimming and other Y activities, my stamp collecting fell by the wayside. I still have the collection to remind me of that period of my life. The pressure to achieve in class increased, as did my loneliness. I grew more distant from my neighborhood friends. I began to stutter and developed a case of acne, bothering me further and mildly depressing me. I soon took steps to remedy both situations. The swimming activities at the local YMCA also brought me into other "Y" activities like the Hi-Y movement. I enjoyed them very much and it provided me with my first ecumenical activity.

The assistant Pastor at St. Mary's Church called me to the rectory one day and pointed out to me that these "Y" activities were essentially Protestant and that I should avoid them. I consulted later with the Pastor, Father Donahue, and he was far less concerned, so I continued my activities at the "Y."

The Other George

George Shattuck, the Principal of Norwich Free Academy, was always friendly toward me when we met at school. One day, I stopped him in the hallway. He smiled and invited me to come into his office right then. I had a difficult time holding back the tears, but I told him that I wanted to stop my stuttering before it worsened. He made an appointment for me to see Mrs. Reed of the Academy staff. I went to see her the next day and started the verbal exercises that she gave me. The next semester I enrolled in a public speaking class. It was great therapy because I could do it anywhere. When I was alone I would repeat the numerous exercises. "The sinking ship sunk," was one of the refrains of the exercises. However, I did not sink thanks to Mrs. Reed. After one year of speech exercises my stuttering disappeared. The following year I went on to win the annual award for public speaking. It was the first school award I had won and remains prominently displayed in my collection to this day.

I always remembered how helpful Mr. Shattuck was. I have tried to be just as responsive with people. Avoiding bureaucratic impediments, cutting through paperwork to the heart of matters and getting things done have always been goals for me.

After Mr. Shattuck helped me to triumph over my stuttering problem, I became more confident and mustered the courage to ask the school doctor about my acne. He recommended that I consult with Dr. Myles Standish, a well-known dermatologist. This was not easy to do, as it involved a trip to Hartford and paying the doctor's fees.

Fortunately, I had just turned sixteen and on that day started working after school at Reid and Hughes Department Store. My weekly pay of ten dollars immediately gave me some cash to pay for an appointment with Dr. Standish in Hartford.

My mother did not drive and my father worked, so I took the bus to Hartford. Dr. Standish prescribed a diet, medication and a weekly X-ray treatment that I could receive at Backus Hospital in Norwich. The weekly treatments cost one dollar. That left two dollars for spending money and seven dollars for my savings account.

Different Roads: Two Good Men

During my time at the Academy, George Shattuck was always friendly and supportive. In him, I felt that I had a friend who could understand the unique challenges that I faced. The two Georges traveled on different roads. Father George Donohue was a devout Catholic; George Shattuck a Protestant believer. Both were kind and helpful to others.

I found early in my life that good people come from all walks of life. The two Georges assisted me at a critical point in my life. I have done my best to do the same with students and young people in need of counsel.

Once I began working at Reid and Hughes, I immediately developed a savings plan. Each Monday on my way from the Academy to the store, I stopped at the Norwich Savings Society and deposited seven or eight dollars. As the balance grew, I became more secure about the prospect of university studies. My family could not give me any financial help. I had studied the catalog from the University of Connecticut, which basically was free for residents of the state. My goal was to save two thousand dollars by the time of graduation to pay for one year of room and board at the university. I hoped that I would receive a scholarship for the remaining years.

I followed George Shattuck's advice and became more active during my senior years in school. Mike Conway, class President, named me editor-in-chief of our class yearbook. It was lots of fun and I had a great staff. But something was bound to suffer in the last semester of my senior year. I was failing physics because I had skipped too many lab exercises. Again I consulted with George Shattuck. He informed me that I could drop the second semester of physics and still have enough credits from my electives to graduate. The trade-off was that I would not receive the prized classical studies diploma but simply a general studies diploma instead, though the official transcript would still indicate that all of my credits were from the classical studies program.

The big mistake I made was not telling my parents. As they sat in the stadium and heard my name called out in the general studies group, my father became visibly upset. He had told all of his friends that his son would be a classical studies graduate. At age fourteen, my mother left the Catholic elementary school in Taftville to assist her family by delivering meals to her father and other members of the family who worked at the local textile mill. My dad, on the other hand, was certified as eligible to attend Norwich Free Academy but, because he had a speech impediment, he was discouraged from doing so.

It was a peculiar atmosphere as the class of 1945 graduated. Some boys were immediately leaving for the freshman summer session at the University of Connecticut. That got them a delay of several months before their induction into the military.

I decided to accept immediate induction into the Army. I knew that the GI Bill was the way for me to get a university education. It is probably one of the best decisions that I ever made.

A Week Later: Into the Army

There was exactly one week between my high school graduation and my induction into the Army. I spent the week saying goodbye to friends; obtaining their addresses and completing the last few pages of the class yearbook.

My mother took my induction especially badly. I remember on one occasion when she wanted to warn me about "the wrong kind of girls" who "hang around" Army camps. She would cry at night. My sisters, Peg and Pat, were twelve and ten; my brother Mark less than a year old. Several boys from the East Side had been killed in the war. It was a close-knit community and we knew all the families. One boyhood friend, Bill De Vito, who had enlisted at seventeen, was killed on naval duty and this greatly distressed my mother, as Bill's mother was her childhood friend from Taftville. The United States was still at war with Japan and her great fear was that I would, as an infantryman, be sent to Japan. She did not know that the war with Japan would be ending two months later.

The day of my departure finally arrived. It was 5:30 in the morning. Ken Botham's dad was waiting for me to join Ken in the car. I tearfully kissed my parents goodbye. My mother held my nine month old brother, Mark, in her arms. My sisters were still sound asleep. My dog, Speck, followed me and wanted to enter the car with me. I also gave him a goodbye hug. As I crossed the street, I saw Aunt Emma peeking out of the window of her second floor apartment. She blew me a kiss.

I climbed into the back of the Bothams' car, trying to hold back the tears. We drove off to the Army depot where I joined another thirty-five men in putting on my first set of Army dungarees. We were then taken to the New London train station.

It was a long two-day train ride to Camp Blanding, Florida. We slept on the floor and I fell asleep with a simple prayer that I would return alive from Army duty so I could benefit from the GI Bill and thus undertake university studies. My prayer was granted. Furthermore, almost two years of military service, mostly with the Army of occupation in Italy, was an excellent experience for me. I learned about different cultures and witnessed the destruction that war can bring. I had no question when I returned to the U.S. that I wanted to learn more about international affairs during my university studies.

My early experiences with love, alienation, and bias were rooted in Norwich and continued during my military service. Aunt Emma however, came from a culture with a very different perspective. My relationship and experience with her left a permanent imprint on my life.

CHAPTER II

AUNT EMMA: PHOTO ALBUMS AND MARIGOLD FLOWERS

MY INTRODUCTION TO WORLD AFFAIRS STARTED IN NORWICH WHILE STILL A schoolboy. I was a stamp collector and, of course, followed the daily newspaper on developments in World War II. The crosscurrents of international politics, ethnic and religious differences took place in my own neighborhood; my own backyard. Aunt Emma was a bridge from innocent boyhood days to my days of military service in Europe.

Aunt Emma lived across the street from my boyhood home in Norwich. Emma, in her early eighties, lived upstairs in a house that her parents, nineteenth-century German immigrants, bought soon after their arrival in the United States around 1880. She was, in a nice way, a character on the street, a retired practical nurse who was frequently working in the flower garden that her father started shortly after his arrival. He brought the flower seeds with them from the beautiful Lake Constance area on the German-Swiss border.

I was helping my mother weed our flower garden when Aunt Emma crossed the street and said that she wanted to talk with both of us. She observed that I seemed very good at cutting grass and working in the flower garden. She wanted to know if I would do the same for her. She paid ten cents an hour. It was 1941. I said yes and began to work that afternoon.

This was the beginning of a romance with someone older than my grandmother.

In the beginning of our relationship, I normally cut her grass and raked the lawn on Saturday afternoons. It took around three hours and I received thirty cents.

Aunt Emma lived on the second floor of the family house. She was able to rent the first floor apartment for twenty-two dollars a month. Along with a small pension of less than twenty-five dollars a month, it gave her a frugal living after she paid the property taxes, utilities, and me. After my first month of cutting grass, she invited me into her apartment and started the tradition of making me a glass of lemonade. In the winter it would be hot chocolate.

Always neatly dressed, Aunt Emma was one of six children in a German immigrant family that settled in a small town in the eastern part of Connecticut. They were faithful members of the local German Lutheran Church. Her family was like most working class families in that area. They either completed their education at the elementary school level or went to secondary commercial or trade school. She was the lucky exception for a girl as she studied practical nursing at the local hospital.

The family was deeply connected with its German heritage. German was the language of her home and this was reinforced with German classes on Saturday at the local German church.

The roots of Norwich go back to the 17th century. The original settlers, after defeating the Mohegan Indians, established a thriving mill town at the convergence of the Shetuket and Yantic Rivers.

The settlers later called Yankees founded the textile and shoe factories. Immigrants and first generation Americans with ancestral roots in Ireland, Poland, Italy and Quebec filled many of the jobs at these factories. A small number of Germans arrived and worked mostly as tradesmen. Emma's family was mostly in this category.

Everyone liked Aunt Emma; she was a nice older lady with snow-white hair and a captivating smile who spent most of her time in the flower garden on her property.

The upstairs flat of four rooms was small but tastefully furnished, mostly with the furniture of her parents. There were two small bedrooms, one where an older sister, Laura, had lived. She died a few years before I started working as a part-time handyman. Aunt Emma had one photo of Laura—a picture taken when she was eighteen—on her bureau.

High School

My job with Aunt Emma started when I began my studies in 1941 at the Norwich Free Academy. When I received the notice of acceptance I showed it to my parents, then went across the street and showed it to Aunt Emma. She was delighted and invited me in for a glass of lemonade. I showed her the academic program and she knew that for the modern language requirement, I had the choice of German or French. Emma's eyes flashed and she urged me to study German.

She took me into the next room and showed me several

shelves of books by German authors. Her favorite book was by Schiller. She went through the closet and pulled out a box of five books for children.

There was her name inscribed on the inside of the cover pages. They were the books from her first five years at the German Saturday school. She said that when I learned some German, she would let me have the books.

I could not bring myself to tell Aunt Emma that I had already selected French. My mother was French Canadian and there was such growing anti-German sentiment that there might not be a sufficient number of students to justify the German course. I learned to refrain from telling her anything negative in order not to hurt the feelings of an older person.

The Photo Albums

One day after my lawn cutting and working in the flower garden, I went to her room for my thirty cents. She was smiling at one of the photo albums. She remarked that 1908 was a great year in her life. In her twenties she had accompanied her parents for a trip to Germany where they stayed for five months in the Lake Constance area on the German-Swiss border.

After working as a practical nurse for seven years she saved enough money to pay for the passage for her parents and herself to the old family home area in Germany.

She gave me the albums to look at. As I flipped through the pages, I saw the photos taken in Germany, mostly family scenes. Then there were several pages of pictures of Emma with a young man. She said, upon my inquiry, "Oh, that is Carl."

Several pages later, there were photos of Emma holding hands with Carl. She was smiling wistfully. I did not say anything.

From then on the photo albums were always on the coffee table next to the sofa which she also used as a bed.

One day, while working in the garden, she asked me to cut for her a particularly beautiful marigold flower. When I was in her room sipping the usual glass of lemonade, I noticed that the marigold was placed inside the photo album next to the photo of Carl! I did not say anything.

When I turned 16 and got my job at the clothing store, I decided to quit my lawn-cutting job for Emma. I lined up a fourteen year old friend in the neighborhood. When I told this to Aunt Emma, she started to cry. Couldn't I do the work in the early evening or even on Sunday? Feelings somewhat remorseful, I said that I would continue working for her and would do it in the early evenings. She then kissed me on the cheek.

War

During my last two years of working for Aunt Emma, the international political situation had changed considerably. Aunt Emma would read the local paper with a magnifying glass. She would talk about the war in terms of her relations to Germany. She seemed lonely to me and she would say, "I hope that they are okay."

Emma was beginning to have hearing problems and asked me to arrange for a bright light to become illuminated when someone rang the doorbell. With the help of my dad, we set out a bright light that went off when the bell was ringing.

As she became more infirm, an increasing number of errands were given to me. I also noticed that she more frequently than ever would look at the photo albums when I came to her room.

It was a rainy day in April when she asked me to go to the flower garden and pick the prettiest marigold. I did and without saying a word, she turned to the photo of Carl, placed the flower next to the photo and left the book open on the coffee table.

For the first time she told me about the sequence of the four photo albums. The first one included old black and white photos of her parents before leaving Germany. They were very badly faded. They all seemed to be happy family scenes.

The second and third albums were scenes from childhood and early youth days in eastern Connecticut. The fourth only had photos from her visit to Germany. Her five-month visit included photos of family and friends. It also included all the photos of Carl.

Christmas is Different Now

It was a week or so before Christmas and I had been cleaning snow from the stairs leading to the apartment. She invited me in and gave me twenty-five cents even though I had only worked an hour.

She poured me a cup of hot chocolate and showed me photos from her album of the Christmas that she spent in Germany. They were the happy scenes of the family of the Christmas tree loaded with many beautiful decorations and of the local Lutheran Church. She was either seated next to or standing with Carl in seven or eight of the photos.

When she finished showing the photos to me she said, "Christmas does not mean much to me now."

I looked at her other table and saw there was only an electric bill—no Christmas cards, no presents.

That evening, I asked my mother to make some fudge. We put the candy in a box, wrapped it in Christmas paper and the next day I gave it to Aunt Emma as my Christmas present.

She opened the box, immediately tasted the fudge and then started to cry. It was her only Christmas present!

I, too, was overwhelmed with a warm feeling for this frail lady. Then she said almost abruptly: she had made a mistake. She should have married Carl and had children. Then she said, looking directly at me, "I would have had a grandson like you and not be alone like I am now."

She then said that religion had kept them apart. Carl was Catholic and she was Lutheran.

Then again looking back directly at me with tears in her eyes, "Do not go through life alone. Marry and have children." I had not thought much about marrying then. But I still remember the words. They came back to me seventeen years later as my then fiancée was marching down the aisle of the church on the arm of her father to marry me.

Christmas, 1944, was followed by my last semester at the Norwich Free Academy. There was a lot of snow in January and in February. Since I worked afternoons and Saturdays at the department store, I performed my working chores for Emma in the early evening or on Sundays. Spring, which came quickly in 1945, was a beautiful Southern New England kind of spring. The city was awash with flowers. I remember one day very well. It was Palm Sunday and I worked all afternoon in the flower garden. Emma spent much of the afternoon with me planting the marigold seeds.

She told me that her father brought the seeds with him from Germany. That day she showed me a big jar where she, like her father, saved the seeds through the fall in winter months, planting her seeds in the spring.

Once the marigolds were in bloom, there was always a vase of them next to the photo albums.

Into the Army

After high school graduation I had a week to prepare for induction into the Army. I went to see Aunt Emma to say goodbye. After drinking the standard glass of lemonade, Aunt Emma said she wanted to show me some letters.

She went to the drawer in her coffee table and took out a bundle of letters, around twenty, and folded envelopes. In every case, the return name and address was the same—Carl.

I wrote down the name and address. She asked me to contact Carl if I should be assigned to Germany. I wondered whether Carl was still alive as he was several years older than Emma, who was then in her early 80's. Not wanting to hurt her feelings, I did not ask the question.

She said to me tactfully that at least now the war with Germany had ended and I would not be "fighting the Germans."

On Thursday morning I said goodbye to my mother and father. As I was closing the door of the Bothams' car I noticed Emma through the ray of light coming from her window. She threw me a kiss and waved goodbye. I waved and was not able to hold back the tears from the other two guys in the car.

I did not know what my future would be after basic training in Camp Blanding, Florida. The time went quickly and in November I was on my way to Italy.

It was an exciting new world for me. Several months after arriving, I was sent to Munich for a training program of three weeks. With the help of a German friend I located a home telephone number listed in Carl's name.

Through my German-speaking friends, I introduced myself as a friend of Carl. The woman responding to my telephone call said, "which one?" I responded, "the friend of Emma." The response was: "He died before the war." The lady volunteered that she was the daughter in law and that her husband, only son of the senior Carl, was killed in the war. There were no other children.

Overwhelmed by the finality of the conversation, I thanked her for the information and went back to my room at the barracks. It was a lonely evening.

How would I tell Emma?

Five months later I was in the United States on home leave. Within minutes of arriving at home, my mother told me that Aunt Emma had passed away several weeks previously. The funeral was bleak, according to my mother. A few people were there. My mother felt that she could not attend because it was a Protestant service. If I had been home I would have advised her to attend the liturgical farewell for a dear friend.

The next day when I returned home from visiting friends, my mother told me that two nieces of Aunt Emma had been to the apartment. They took a few items of furniture but they put all of her books into a trashcan.

I quickly walked across the street. There were the German books, including the early readers in the trashcan.

Suddenly, upon looking through the trash, I became overwhelmed with the emotion as I saw in the bottom of the can the four photo albums. They had been evidently thrown into he trashcan with haste. Some of the photos had fallen out. And there was one with Emma holding hands with Carl.

I was shocked. No one cared; no one wanted the photo albums! I took the photo of Emma and Carl holding hands;

momentarily placed it in my pocket. Then I pulled it out and placed it back into the trashcan. It was not mine to keep. It had not been my romance. It belonged to the memory of Emma.

I ran across the street, and as I was entering my family home through the front door, I saw my mother's Marigold flower garden. They were from the seeds that Emma gave to me. They originally came from the collection started by Aunt Emma's father.

This was the heritage that would be preserved. Emma's memory for me would be the beautiful flower garden. Emma was gone, Carl had passed away. There were no children from either of them.

I realized then how much I loved Aunt Emma. I think of her every time I see a garden of marigold flowers.

CHAPTER III

THE ARMY: NEW HORIZONS

As the troop ship approached Naples, Italy in mid-November 1945, I saw the graphic destruction of war. I said a private prayer of thanksgiving for safe arrival and for the end of the war. With the army gear on our backs, on leaving the ship we were immediately placed on the train for the long ride to Leghorn. The war was over. I was part of the Army of occupation.

The train stopped at various points where local people had a variety of goods to sell. For the first time I tasted the delicious oranges of Sicily. Once we arrived at the Leghorn train station, I again saw massive destruction all around us. I went to bed that evening wondering what the new life would be like. I also had flashes of the first scenes of the brutality of the war in two of Italy's major cities.

Several times on the eleven-day voyage of the troop ship across the Atlantic Ocean, I wondered about my decision to accept immediate induction into the Army and not postpone it by attending classes at the University of Connecticut. The ship was packed with soldiers; we hit a storm for two days and I was seasick. The latrines were blocked and I had latrine duty for one full day.

After several days in a temporary facility, I was assigned to a unit in Tirena on the outskirts of Leghorn. Following a few days of rushing and waiting I was called in by the Commanding Officer and told that I was a candidate for the assignment of Information and Education assistant. I was sent to headquarters in Leghorn and met the officers responsible for the I & E program for this part of Italy.

The officers were all university graduates and the enlisted men normally had at least one year of university studies. In the early part of the interviewing there seemed to be a stumbling block about my lack of any university studies. However, I had a good interview with the Colonel in charge. He endorsed my appointment as the I & E assistant for my unit.

Our organization was housed in what had been a school on the shores of the Mediterranean in Tirena. It was a beautiful, resort-like location with a waterfront for boats. It was ideal for swimming in the summer.

Our company was composed primarily of senior veterans who had spent several years in combat, mostly in Italy and North Africa. I was a member of a smaller contingent of new arrivals who were mostly 18 years old.

A major task given to me was to establish and monitor the lending library. I also posted the information on the I & E excursions in Italy and the one-week tours of Switzerland, Austria, Germany, France and England.

By Thanksgiving I felt that I was in paradise. I was the technician in charge of the library and three-day tours in Italy and one week tours outside of Italy. I had already arranged and participated in three-day weekend trips to Florence, Siena, Lucca and Pisa.

Christmas in Rome

After only six weeks in Italy, the Commanding Officer authorized a one-week excursion to Rome for Christmas and New Year. For me it was a work assignment and the trip to Rome, like most of the other ones, did not count for leave time.

Andy, Joe, John and several other Catholics stayed close to me on this trip. With the assistance of the Catholic Chaplain we arranged a trip to the Vatican. A highlight was the papal audience. All the U.S. military personal were placed together in the audience hall and Pope Pius XII spoke to us in English. It was an unforgettable moment. Little did I sense when I first met Pope Pius XII in December 1945, that forty-four years later I would be presenting my credentials to his successor as the U.S. Ambassador.

Not all the G.I.s on the Rome trip spent their time sightseeing or visiting the Vatican. Rome had an active prostitution community. In leaving the military facility, we were given a prophylactic kit, which contained a condom in case we should have sex. When we returned there was a "pro room" where we were expected to apply a preventive medicine just in case we had sex.

It was probably the only way to reduce the incidence of venereal disease, as there was a high incidence of promiscuous sex among G.I.'s and other soldiers with the local civilians. The same was true when the German soldiers occupied Rome.

I made the resolution to obey the Commandments on this issue. It was not always easy.

German POW's

The German prisoners of war housed in a camp across from ours in Tirena were assigned duty with our unit. Hans was my assistant in the library. He was in his mid-twenties and was born in Prussia. His previous duty was in France and Poland. He was captured while serving in northern Italy. We had plenty of discussions—in many ways he was still a fascist.

Another German POW was assigned to maintain the tennis courts. Wolfgang came from Westphalia and was actually a very good tennis player. In the spring of 1946 he gave me lessons almost daily. I also saw Wolfgang at Mass on Sundays as the German POW Catholics sometimes used the local Catholic Church, which was also our chapel.

I would give them items like after-shave lotion, candy bars and razor blades. One day Lt. Erickson, the Executive Officer of our unit, came to see me in the library. He closed the door and screamed that I was "too friendly" with the German POW's. He threatened to take away my I & E assignment and give me KP duty (cleaning the kitchen). After that I was more restrained in my contacts with them although I continued to "slip" them items from the PX.

The German POW camp was desolate and the men there had no knowledge of when they would be repatriated to Germany. There was consequently a high rate of escapes. Both Hans and Wolfgang were among those who escaped. They gave me hints that they would do that. A day or so before they escaped, they came to thank me and to say "Aufwiedersehen."

Actually I heard from them later in life and visited Wolfgang at his home in Nordwalde. The first time was with Margaret and we discussed our time together; he as a POW and I as a member of the Army of occupation.

The war left bitterness on both sides but I was interested in spreading the process of reconciliation, despite my limited contacts.

Lt. Erickson continued to harass me for my friendship with German POW's. He had all the usual epithets for them: Nazi bastards, Prussian killers, etc. His reputation at Leghorn headquarters was not good and when he complained about me, the I & E bosses praised my work. Their influence protected me.

He was also anti-religious and made inappropriate remarks about Catholic beliefs. When it was announced that he was being repatriated to the U.S., I sighed with relief.

On the morning of his departure, I did not want to salute him so I stayed in my quarters. I was able to see him as he climbed into the Jeep that would take him to the troop ship in Leghorn Harbor. He had the usual army gear bag. No one was there to assist him and no one was there to salute or wave goodbye. He was a lonely figure. At that moment I actually felt sorry for him.

Andy had a cousin named Luisa who lived near Genoa. She came to our unit several times and we visited her. It was soon apparent to me that she had a "crush" on me. We dated but I pulled back because she was serious and a very good person. Luisa was also seven years older than me. I had no intention of becoming involved in a serious relationship. We stayed in contact by letters. She never married. Forty-four years later when I returned to Italy as U.S. Ambassador to the Vatican with Margaret, we visited her. Margaret and I slept in the same bed that I did when I first visited her with Andy.

We talked on the phone. She was a lonely figure. When she passed away I received the news after her funeral with some sadness. It brought back both the good memories that we had together and the sad images that I saw of her life when four decades later, I returned to Italy.

Visits to Austria, Germany and Switzerland

In the spring of 1946 I was sent on temporary duty for three weeks to Austria and Germany. My first stop was Vienna where I was again shocked by the destruction. I had seen the pre-war photos in a book about Vienna. People were still clearing the rubble and carting it away in wheel barrows.

The famous Cathedral in Vienna had suffered, but it still stood. Several in my group who were Catholics lit a candle at the one altar that was not damaged. Later the Austrian guide, when we went into the canteen for a snack, asked me in a whisper if I could bring a sandwich or two, which she would save and take home to her family. I violated the regulations and brought her two toasted cheese sandwiches and several candy bars.

The occupation of the city was divided in four zones: British, French, Soviet and U.S. I had a funny feeling riding in the bus through the Soviet zone. I thought: allies in one year, adversaries in the next.

From Austria we took the train to Munich where I was stationed for two weeks. It was there that I fulfilled Aunt Emma's wish for me to find Carl.

In Munich I also contacted the cousins of another POW friend from Leghorn. I gave him a letter and answered questions on the POW living conditions. He met me in the city near the building where I was taking the orientation and invited me to his home for dinner. I remember taking the taxi that evening. I stayed for several hours enjoying the dinner and chatting with his mother and sister. His father had been killed on the Russian front. His brother was captured by the Russians and was still a POW. I could see that their German mother was sad about the deaths in her family and the situation of her son in a POW camp. German mothers and American mothers all felt the same pain.

I left his home for the short walk to a taxi stand and was stopped by an M.P. patrol. I was asked for a pass. I had none but fortunately I had travel orders with me. The M.P. Sgt. told me that I needed to have a pass to be in that area. After a few worrying moments, he told me to get in the back seat and drove me to where I was staying.

The temporary duty in Munich was intended to familiarize us with the correspondence courses offered by the U.S. Army to all servicemen.

While the training program was interesting, I continued to be shocked by the massive destruction of German cities and the destitute appearance of the German people. I made an overnight trip to Cologne. The destruction there was even worse. It was winter and many of the people in the streets had inadequate clothing.

A week after I returned to Leghorn. I was assigned to a one-week tour group of Switzerland. What a contrast! The massive destruction in Austria and Germany and the "music box" serenity of Switzerland. This was my second visit to Switzerland. I took a day off and visited the University of Geneva to see about the possibility of staying in Europe for my education. I was disappointed by the big lecture classes and, what seemed to me, the depersonalized atmosphere.

In Zurich while visiting a park I had a first experience: a direct invitation by an older Swiss gay man to visit his apartment. I declined the invitation. It was not the last one that I would decline in my youth.

The summer of 1946 was consumed by three-day weekend passes to all the leading cities of Italy where there were military hotels that gave us free room and board. Every once in a while I would pinch myself. Was I having a dream? I was on a grand tour of Europe while building up credits for the G.I. Bill of Rights.

The Black Market

The black market was a fact of life in Italy in 1946. While all sales through the black market were illegal, there was a de facto acceptance that it was okay to sell one carton of cigarettes which was the weekly ration. I did not smoke and sold mine. I was consequently able to save a good part of my monthly paycheck. I was saving for the next big focus in my life: university studies.

There was one offer that was tempting but I turned it down in regard to the black market. The I & E program worked closely with the sports division. I had the key to the warehouse for our unit. A senior level Italian employee approached me about tennis and basketball shoes. I would get half the income that he would receive from the sale on the black market. I declined the invitation. While selling my weekly cigarette ration did not disturb me, the idea of stealing certainly did.

A month or so later a soldier in my unit working with a 1st lieutenant stole a major haul of athletic equipment. They were caught, court marshaled and spent a few months in the local military jail. I visited my friend Bill—he was later honorably discharged, but carried the court martial stigma the rest of his life. I thanked God I didn't give into the temptation.

In September 1946, I was transferred to the Peninsula Base section headquarters in Leghorn. I had just been promoted to Corporal and the new assignment was a step up. I had the same duties—to oversee the library and to sign up G.I.'s for excursions and tours.

I managed a trip to England, where I also made a five-day private excursion to Dublin. It was not authorized and I made the crossing from Liverpool to Dublin without a passport. I was in uniform and the customs officer admitted me with a smile. I had a great urge to at least touch the soil of Ireland. I remembered the stories of my grandfather, Philip G. Melady, about his boyhood days in Ireland. I met several Irish guys my age and visited several pubs and the university. I found it to be a neat possibility as there would be no language problems. There also seemed to be a total absence of communism and anti-Americanism.

There was another trip to France. There was a special office at the University of Paris for foreign students to inquire about studies there. The strong factors of communism and anti-Americanism discouraged me from pursuing university studies in Paris.

Need for Service

In Leghorn, near the base, there were an increasing number of teenage boys who had been abandoned by their families or who never had a family. I talked to the Catholic Chaplain, who was involved with a project known as "The Shoe Shine Boys

Fund," for boys who were either orphaned or abandoned by single mothers. They waited outside of military camps, as it was an easy way for the American soldiers to keep their boots shined.

The Fund would provide shelter under Catholic auspices, buy clothes, etc. and, more importantly, provided an alternative to hanging around military camps. Some of these boys would be taken advantage of by prostitutes and given a tip for each "client" they produced.

There were collection boxes and I placed them, at the Chaplain's request, in the cafeteria, recreation room and at the bar. I ran into some trouble with the Master Sgt. in charge of our unit. He told me that he did not trust priests and that I should remove the collection boxes from these places.

I had no choice but to remove them. However, I remained active in the project and arranged for a news article on the fund in our weekly Army newspaper.

Thoughts About the Future

Christmas 1946 came and I spent it with John and Andy in Florence. They were thinking about their future. I tried to convince them to take advantage of the G.I. Bill and to go to a university.

Shortly after New Year's Day, those of us who were enlisted with the Army in June 1945 were informed that we were eligible for repatriation to the U.S. in February 1947.

I thought about it and concluded that arriving in the U.S. in February would be too late to start at the university. Furthermore, I was still thinking about doing my university work in Europe. I therefore took my discharge in Italy, found employment at the Army Exchange Service and spent the months of March, April and May visiting universities in Italy. By May I decided that I would pursue studies in the U.S. I returned home on a freighter, which took around twenty or so passengers. The ship left Genoa in mid June and arrived ten days later in New York.

Before leaving, I telephoned Luisa and invited her to Genoa. We had dinner together and I gave her flowers. She cried and I felt sorry that I invited her, as I could not return the love that she felt for me.

I had spent twenty months abroad. I had been eighteen when I reported for basic training in Camp Blanding, Florida in June, 1945. Now, at twenty, I had a great experience while growing from an adolescent into a young man.

My arrival in New York City by ship was memorable. All the other passengers were Europeans immigrating to the U.S. They all had relatives and friends waiting for them. No one was there for me. It was a lonely feeling, but I knew the circumstances of my family in Norwich would have made it difficult for anyone to come to New York. My father was working the second shift at a trucking company, and my mother did not know how to drive. Within an hour of getting off the boat I was at the train station.

The train ride from New York to Norwich gave me a chance to reflect on the future. Once I arrived in New London, I took a taxi to Norwich. I had telephoned about the approximate time that I would be arriving. The door was open, as my mother never locked it.

My dad was sleeping and my mother arrived a few minutes later with Mark in the carriage (he was two and a half). My sisters Peg and Pat were at school. We had a good reunion, but my dad had to leave for his second shift work.

Thus began about two months for me in Norwich until I left for the school just before Labor Day. The first day home would be like the rest of the summer. I would have difficulty in reconnecting with my boyhood hometown. It was a dilemma. I was back, alive and well in my hometown. But I wanted to leave as I had the great desire for university studies.

Focus on the Family Situation

My dad was working the night shift at the trucking company, loading and unloading merchandise. He would leave for work around 6 p.m., return around 5 a.m. His total income was around seventy-five dollars a week.

After a few days at home, I could sense that the money situation was tight. My father had an old 1930 car. I bought them a very good second-hand Chevrolet. My mother had been in the habit of making all the clothes for my sisters. As they were becoming teenagers, they wanted more exciting clothes. But on the family's income, that was difficult.

Since I had been accepted as a student at Duquesne, I knew that I had a university to attend. The universities were packed and it was difficult for returning G.I.'s to find acceptances at institutions they wanted to attend. I was very pleased with the knowledge that in September I would be at a university.

I spent the first three weeks visiting relatives and friends. I was quite excited about my great European experience. I soon discovered that this was not true of many of my friends and relatives.

I re-established contact with Kathryn. We had dated in my senior year at the Academy and corresponded while I was in the Army. It was difficult for me to focus on any kind of relationship for two reasons: I was beginning to think that I might consider the priesthood for a vocation. Also, I was beginning to feel that I would not make Norwich my home.

By mid-July I was waiting impatiently for September 1, when I would leave for Pittsburgh and Duquesne University. But an incident occurred that gave me something outside of myself to concentrate on.

In mid-July I met Dr. Bill Driscoll, a boyhood friend of my dad from Jewett City. Bill, after attending elementary school with my dad, went to the Academy, then medical school and then established his medical practice in Norwich. His son Will was a classmate of mine at the Academy.

Bill told me that he bumped into my dad and wanted to alert me that my dad, then forty-seven, was a candidate for a nervous breakdown. He pointed out to me that the hard labor work he did as he was approaching fifty isolated him from social contacts. He noted that furthermore, my father carried the resentment of being born with a speech impairment.

In a way Dr. Driscoll's diagnosis confirmed my own feeling. I discussed it first with my mother and then with both of them. We decided to look for a "mom and pop" type small business which they could buy. Most of August was spent looking at places for sale. I would identify the opportunities during the week and on the weekends we would go together to see them.

We looked at a bakery in Mystic, grocery stores and liquor stores in Norwich. My parents were slow to move on this project. One problem was money. They had around $5,000 in savings. Most of the opportunities seemed to be at the $10,000 level.

September 1 came around and there was no change in the situation of my parents and family. When they drove me to the

New London train station I worried about the future. But they were happy that their son was starting his university studies.

On the subject of my parents seeking a new situation, I stayed in contact with them during my first year at the university. I was having a very enjoyable time, but I always thought of them. I was home for Christmas and could see that my dad was in dire need of a change.

I was not able to come home immediately after the academic year ended in June, as I had to spend six weeks at ROTC summer camp in Fort Bragg, North Carolina. As soon as I returned in August I started on the project of finding a business for them. The four weeks went quickly. We saw a dozen or so "mom and pop" stores. Toward the end of my stay in Norwich, one good possibility developed. A package store was available. The price was $10,000. My folks had $5,000 in savings; they could borrow $3,000 on their house. They needed and additional $2,000 and I loaned them that amount from my savings. I had saved around $3,500 from high school work and the Army and was pleased to give them a helping hand.

I left for Duquesne and Pittsburgh feeling that my folks were on another path. The new business was good for my dad. He and my mother worked the store for twenty-seven years and sold it when they decided to retire.

Within several years after entering the business my dad developed a drinking problem. At first no one would discuss it. When we did my mother took the lead in confronting Dad. The results were remarkable. He stopped drinking "cold turkey" and never again touched a drop. There were numerous family events including the baptisms of all of his grandchildren. He, once committed, never touched an alcholic drink.

I knew that it was a difficult thing to do and I admired him for his action. His life was not an easy one. We never, in my opinion, realized the impact of being born with a speech impediment that no one attempted to have corrected, or the difficulty of coming from a home where his father and mother were separated because of his father's drinking problems.

When he died in 1979 I regretted not having had the opportunity of knowing him better when I was young and at home, as he was working most of the time. Starting at eighteen, I was never home except for brief visits. When he attended the swearing-in ceremonies for me as Ambassador and later the inaugural ceremonies when I became a university President, I knew that he was proud of me.

On a few occasions when in the Norwich area I visit the cemetery where Dad and Mom are buried. St. Joseph's Cemetery is located on the fork of the road. One leads to Taftville where Mother was born and the other to Jewett City where Dad was born. It was a final resting-place for so many Catholic families who had roots in neighboring Taftville and Jewett City as well as Norwich.

Their union gave a solid dedicated home to their four children. They reflected their culture—working class Catholics — and through it gave us all their love.

CHAPTER IV

University Studies: At Long Last

Following service in the U.S. Army I began my university studies at Duquesne University in Pittsburgh in 1947. I did not give much thought to the process of selecting a university. I wanted to leave the New England area and have an experience in another part of the country. The GI Bill gave me the freedom to do that. The acceptance from the University of Connecticut that I received when I graduated from the Norwich Free Academy two years before was no longer important to me.

It was the Catholic factor that influenced me to select Duquesne. I had an inner feeling that I should enter the priesthood. At Duquesne I arranged to take as many courses in philosophy and religious studies as was possible.

I always seemed to be in a rush. I had "lost" two years from being in the military service. By taking the maximum number of courses and attending a summer session at Temple University, I was able to complete the four-year program in three years. I never analyzed why I always felt that I was in a "hurry."

My activities included debating, student council and the National Federation of Catholic College Students. It was a totally different experience for me from high school. At the Norwich Free Academy, it was study, study and study; after school and on Saturday, it was work. This schedule left no time for associating with my peer group. High school was in many ways a lonely period in my life.

Studies at Duquesne were entirely different. I was comfortable with the academic schedule—A's and B's were my principle grades and I had plenty of time for student life as the GI Bill allowance and the ROTC stipend gave me a comfortable spending budget. My three years at Duquesne were very enjoyable.

Religious Pluralism

During my student days at Duquesne I thought about entering the priesthood. It was during this time that I also had my first encounter with intolerance. In my political science and philosophy courses I was faced with the teaching that the Catholic Church was the "only true Church." It was not possible for me to accept that teaching.

My rejection of it was personal rather than intellectual. I could not believe that God, as a result of this teaching, would exclude so many from eventual union with Him. Several years later, as a graduate student at a Catholic University of America, I would encounter the same challenge on a more serious level.

When it came to social activities I was more aggressive in speaking out against religious intolerance. Soon after my arrival at Duquesne, I was invited to join several different fraternities. Most of them had a religious requirement: you had to be a practicing Catholic.

I had several friends who were not Catholic and consequently it was difficult to find a fraternity for them. In this case, I found friends who felt as I did: there should be fraternities and social organizations open to all regardless of their religion.

Gary Orr, John Miller, Bob Reno and others joined me in organizing the Bachelor's club with Father Vernon Gallagher, Vice President of the University, as our Chaplain. There was no religious requirement. By the end of the first year we had twenty-five members, mostly Catholics, but also Protestants and Jews.

The enthusiasm of a "new group" on campus was short lived. At the end of one year, the Club applied for official recognition from the University. To my great disappointment, we were turned down. Why? The rumor circulating within twenty-four hours of the rejection was that we had no religious identification.

I organized a campaign to obtain recognition. Our main theme was that there should be a fraternity that was open to everyone, regardless of their religious identification. It was my first experience of working through the structures. We presented our case in a written document and then met with the academic officials.

As I learned from a member of the University Executive Committee, one high ranking official had concluded that our group, instead of being open to all, was actually inspired by some anti-religious feelings. We won in our lobbying efforts and, on the second try, we were recognized by the university.

I had similar challenges with the National Federation of Catholic College Students (NFCCS). I pushed for including all Catholics in the Organization. I was President of the Chapter at

Duquesne University. Several of my friends who were in the leadership groups with me felt that we should separate the good Catholics from the "bad ones." I was uncomfortable with that position. This was the beginning of my belief that we should be compassionate about all Catholics.

I disliked the idea of separating one group of Catholics from another. My belief was that if a Catholic believed in the Church, then he was a Catholic. Any attempt to classify him disturbed me. This, in my opinion, was the prerogative of God.

The matter came up in the student elections. At the election following communion breakfast, my nomination for the presidency was challenged on the basis that I was "too friendly with the playboys on campus" and was known for hanging out with the "drinking set."

I decided at that moment to react to the charge. It was my first speech on tolerance. I spoke about personal charity and avoiding the appearance of self-righteousness. I was elected president by a substantial margin and from that day I remain uncomfortable with any kind of self-righteousness.

My other major activity was the debating team. We had an excellent coach, Professor John Desmond. At the end of the first year, I was elected captain. I was awarded the Medal for Excellence in Debating at graduation.

I was twenty-three on the day in 1950 when I graduated from Duquesne University. While still not sure of the direction of my career, I knew then that becoming a priest was not in my destiny. What would I do?

Government and politics appealed to me to me and I selected the Catholic University of America. The acceptance letter for the graduate program in the international relations arrived the weekend of my graduation.

My mother and my sister Peg came to Pittsburgh for my

graduation. It was a great family moment. My Dad, sister, Pat, and brother Mark remained in Norwich. My first step in university studies had been accomplished.

The undergraduate years were full of sweet memories. It was such a pleasant difference from high school. I was comfortable with the studies and had no money problems. The stuttering and acne problems faded away and the peer relationships were very good. And I had a sense of my future career: life in the public square and some sort of public service.

My interest in the priesthood made me reluctant to develop any kind of relationship with a girl at Duquesne. I never had any such attachment there. That aspect of my life was cleared up and I felt free to cultivate such relationships when I started my studies at the Catholic University of America.

My last twenty-four hours at Duquesne were ones that left a permanent imprint on me. I was saying goodbye to friends; packing my suitcases and wondering about the future. It was in some ways a lonely feeling. I had become attached to the University and its surroundings. It was my home. What would the future bring?

The Catholic University of America

The three summer months of 1950 in an Army reserve camp were full of questions. Would I be called up for military service in the Korean War? There was only a gap of five years between the end of the World War II war and the Korean War. I actually resented it partially because I might become involved and also because I wondered, is war the only solution to mankind's problems?

I started my September classes at Catholic University with

enthusiasm. I was studying for an M.A. in international relations and was delighted to be preparing for a career in relations between states, international organizations, and international economies.

Graduate students in all faculties numbered over two thousand five hundred, and I became involved in efforts to establish a lecture series and some appropriate social functions. The Graduate Student Council was formed and I was elected its first president in 1951.

Conservative or Liberal: Which way?

In international relations my leanings were in the conservative direction. The Soviet takeover of the Eastern and Central European countries troubled me. The Marxist strength in Eastern Europe and the Communist takeover in China influenced me to sign up with the Republican Party.

I came from a democratic background. My mother and father, like most members of the working class in Connecticut, were Democrats. Sometimes I was confused on the matter, as I felt in my heart that the Democratic Party was more sympathetic to the working people—and that was my background. But as a graduate student fully immersed in international studies, I concluded that the Republican Party was more sensitive to the dangers of worldwide Communism, and so I became a lifelong member of the Republican Party.

One of my closest friends on the faculty was Father Francis J. Powers, C.S.V. He was a superb teacher and a fine priest. He was also a liberal Democrat and frequently teased me about my Republican leanings.

I received an M.A. in international relations in June 1952.

This time my dad drove from Norwich with my sister Peg for the graduation ceremonies. My mother remained at home taking care of the store. I worked at the National Security Agency for the summer and was able to save a good part of my salary to help defray tuition costs. My G.I. Bill benefits ended in 1952.

I had my first political experience in 1952. General Eisenhower was the Republican candidate for President and I was an active member of Young Republican Club in Washington D.C. and emerged as chairman of the local chapter of Students For Eisenhower. The elections of 1952 were for me mostly fun. The other experiences that year brought me into contact with the reality of the racial divide.

Benedict Njoku from Nigeria was a graduate student in history and lived on campus in Graduate Hall. One weekend, several of us, including Ben, walked to the neighborhood and stopped at a drugstore in Brookland. I still remember the shock when I heard the words, "we do not serve colored people here." After a few seconds of reflections, I said, "you will either serve all of us or we will all leave."

The waitress would not serve Ben, so we left. The bar across the street would serve Ben, provided that he stayed with us. We had to accept that compromise.

As a student living on the campuses of Catholic University, I was protected from the racial segregation in Washington, D.C. Students of all races attended the University and lived in the dormitories. In many ways the Catholic University campus in the 1950's was like a global village: all races living in the same community.

In the spring of 1953 the School of Law was having a dinner down at the Wardman Park. In this case we were told the same thing-two African-American students from the University came with their dates to the hotel. They were stopped at the hotel and our response was: you take us all or we all leave. Our group of six couples left but the other students did not join us.

In both cases I could see the hurt on the faces of my classmates. I have always felt strongly since then that racism remains one of the great curses of our world.

The Supreme Court decision came that year outlawing segregation in public facilities.

The combination of these racial experiences, plus the starting of the independence movement in Black Africa energized my interest for a career in African affairs.

The International Relations Club

Since I was majoring in international relations, I was an active member of the International Relations Club. The moderator was a refugee professor, Dr. William Roberts. After several incidents where there were disagreements on the program, George Parker, Timothy May, Don Kommers and I initiated a petition to the Vice Rector urging that Dr. Roberts be replaced by Father Francis J. Powers, who was very popular with students.

Little did we know that a minor student affair would reveal intrigues in the University administration. Several members of the administration who represented the old guard feared Fr. Powers as a rival. In addition to his professional credentials, he was an articulate advocate of Papal social teachings.

An investigation was initiated by the Dean, Monsignor Campbell, and I was placed under heavy pressure to say that Fr. Powers inspired us to circulate the petitions to have him replace Dr. Robers. It was a kangaroo court. The students, including myself, were reprimanded. The group who brought the charge against us that resulted in the "investigation" wanted us expelled but we were "slapped on the fingers." The Vice Rector advised me to complete my studies and to launch my career.

A few years later Dr. Roberts, who moved totally to the extreme right in his interpretations of international relations, brought an unsuccessful suit against the University and left the University in early retirement a bitter man. Later in life when I would see him at university alumni affairs, I felt sorry for him. His suit was a source of embarrassment for the University. His actions left him with very few friends.

The more profound impact on me was the open intrigues and the nastiness that existed among a few of the clergy and laity at the University. I learned a lesson for the future: not all clergy practice what they preach.

This was a lesson that helped me throughout the rest of my life. The clergy of the Church was and is made up of mostly very good and dedicated men. From time to time I would encounter others who did not measure up to the high standards of the Church. But I was inspired by those who were examples of Christian love and compassion and I ignored the others.

Father John Courtney Murray: An Inspiration

As president of the graduate student council I arranged for visits of speakers to the campus. They were all from the area of public affairs. We had an especially active season in 1952-53. Guests included Clare Booth Luce, then the newly appointed Ambassador to Italy, Illinois Senator Douglas and the Ambassador of Ireland.

I invited the Jesuit theologian Father John Courtney Murray to give a lecture on religious freedom, which he accepted. I was subsequently invited to the Vice Rector's office and informed that the Church did not approve of Father Murray's teachings on religious freedom. I was told that I should cancel the invitation.

I explained the circumstances to Father Murray and he said, "Tom, I understand. I still have some more work to do and believe that my next publication will help to establish the credibility of my positions on religious freedom." He advised me not to make a fuss about his not being welcome on the campus.

While I was disappointed with the Catholic University decision, I was very impressed by Father Murray's attitude. He had no desire to create a stir on the university campus and to take a confrontational position against official church teaching. Father Murray preferred to do his research and to establish the credibility of his position. He worked through established Church structures.

Within a few years Father Murray saw his recommendation accepted and incorporated by Vatican Council II. Eleven years after his invitation was withdrawn from the graduate student lecture series at Catholic University, he had the joy of being at the Vatican on December 7, 1965, when the Vatican II document on religious freedom was issued.

John Courtney Murray's way of seeking change was an inspiration to me. His model was one that I have tried to follow. Unfortunately, some contemporary advocates of change have not followed the "Murray way" of initiating change.

The "Murray way" requires patience and respect for the good will of the organization where you are seeking changes. Murray's advocacy was more credible because of his obvious loyalty to the Church in his search for changes in

Church policy.

Over the decades I have worked with my co-religionists to effect change in administrative areas. Working with people and sharing a vision has been effective and rewarding.

This sometimes means that there is a natural tension among well-meaning groups. The opposing points of view within the Catholic community were clarified in 1965 by the Vatican in the document on religious freedom.

The forces who did not accept Father Murray's interpretation later, for the most part, accepted the interpretation of the Vatican document as this was now the official teaching of the Church. This is the benefit of having a central authority.

It was a very fortunate development because slightly more then a decade later, Pope John Paul II was to make religious freedom a cornerstone in his successful campaign against the Soviet communist control of the Eastern European countries.

Call to Active Duty: Rumors on Campus

In the summer of 1953, after passing the comprehensive exams I was called to active duty as a 2nd Lt. in the reserve. I received a deferment of one year to complete my Ph.D. studies.

When I told this to my Dean, Dr. Joseph Neusse, he remarked that very few students completed their doctoral dissertations in two semesters (eight months)! I did not have much choice. In order to do that, I knew that I would need to isolate myself from all distractions. I moved into an attic room half a block away from the campus and in eight months I completed the dissertation; it was accepted and three weeks later, I passed the Ph.D. oral exam.

May through June 1954 were eventful months. My goal of obtaining a Ph.D. was accomplished; and much to my surprise, the call to active duty was cancelled. I was told that the Army had a surplus of junior officers.

But several of my friends told me about a disturbing rumor on campus in regard to my completing my Ph.D. thesis in eight months. The rumor was that my director, Dr. Joseph Sulkowski, and the reader, Father Francis J. Powers were "easy" on me. Michael Szas was identified as the student who reported to University authorities that for both my M.A. thesis and the Ph.D. dissertation I had a professional who wrote the final draft. Both my M.A. thesis and my Ph.D. dissertation were my own work, from the research to the final written document.

I was irritated by this malicious rumor. I wanted to confront Szas directly, but since the information was "leaked" to me by a member of the University administration, I could not do that. Father Powers urged me also not to seek revenge. He pointed out that the student was an unhappy and unsuccessful one and was most likely envious. It was another brush with envy. It would not be the last!

Many years later, Szas approached me for help. He was in difficult financial circumstances. I gave him a small amount. When I learned about his death while on a sabbatical in Rome in 2001 I regretted not having forgiven him.

During my four years as a graduate student at the Catholic University of America, I defined myself both in terms of religion and politics. I was stronger than ever in my commitment to the Catholic faith, the religion of my ancestors. It has remained very much a part of me. Later, when terms like "conservative" or "liberal" were used with great ease, I remained Catholic without a preceding adjective, believing in the institution and its core teachings.

My graduate student days also defined my political views. I was conservative in foreign policy. On the domestic scene the basic teachings of the Church on the family, education, and the dignity of the human being closely allied me with the Republican Party. These two commitments never changed. I will always be grateful for the opportunity I had of spending seven years in studies in my formative years at two great universities.

CHAPTER V

BABY JOE, HARVARD AND THE EPISCOPAL CHURCH

IN THE SUMMER MONTHS OF 1954, AS I WAS PUTTING THE FINAL TOUCHES on my doctoral dissertation at the Catholic University of America, I was at the same time looking for my first professional job. Since my graduate studies were in government and economics, I was focusing on these areas for employment.

During the academic year, while a student at the Catholic University of America, I worked at the National Shrine of the Immaculate Conception on a part-time basis. Starting in the summer of 1954 I worked full time until October, when I started work with the U.S. Foreign Operations Administration.

There had been a downturn in the economy and jobs were difficult to find. The Eisenhower administration was placing greater emphasis on trade rather than aid in its international assistance program. In August 1954 the newspapers reported on a program where the Foreign Operations Administration would recruit eighteen recent university graduates who would be designated as trade and investment assistants. They would work with the United States Aid Missions to assist the developing countries to transform their economies into investment and trade friendly environments.

Over two hundred men applied for the eighteen slots. The competition was tough. I was interviewed and several weeks later, the phone rang and a man with a distinct Texas accent gave me the good news that I had been accepted in the program. He told me that I should report to his office the following day at 10 a.m.

Greeting me the following morning was a very overweight man with a friendly smile and a gregarious personality. Joe Lafayette Hill had been a successful lawyer who had made the right investments with his wife's fortune. He turned old money into lots of new money. He also served in the Texas State Senate.

Now in the shadows of his life, Mr. Hill, a lifelong Democrat, had campaigned for Dwight Eisenhower, the Republican presidential candidate, in Texas. He was rewarded with a job in Washington, D.C.

Joe Hill was attracted to a program that would help other people to help themselves. He was fundamentally ill at ease with aid programs, but this one appealed to him philosophically and he was enthusiastic in support of it.

We had a five-month training program. Mr. Hill invited me to serve as his special assistant, in addition to participating in the program. The five months went by quickly. Several times a week I would go with him to his apartment at the hotel next to our office building. I met Mrs. Hill, who was frail and obviously not in good health.

They both loved a brand of New Orleans coffee. She always served it with a few sugar cookies.

Mr. Hill soon confided in me that his wife Ethel was seriously ill and that it was a matter of "six or seven months" before she would pass away. He wondered out loud to me, what would he do after Ethel passed away?

Sent to Ethiopia and Returned

During the Christmas season of 1954, when the training was coming to an end, Mr. Hill gave me several options. My special assistant role to Mr. Hill was in addition to participating in the training program with the other seventeen trainees. I was given one grade higher (around $1,500 a year) for the extra work. This stimulated some envy and jealousy. They were factors that I learned to live with. I selected Ethiopia and arrived there in February of 1955. A normal assignment of two years was cut down to one year, as the United States government was not pleased with the almost total lack of implementation of U.S. recommendations for creating a more attractive investment climate.

Upon returning to Washington in February 1956, I was again assigned to Mr. Hill. His wife was in the final stages of a terminal illness and had returned to Texas. She had lingered longer than expected.

Since he had been a state Senator for many years, most of his Texan friends who visited him called him, "Senator." I either used "Senator" or "Mr." I never used his first name.

Joe Hill was at this time in his career a lonely man. He would invite me to have dinner with him at least once a week.

I noticed that his focus was increasingly on me. The one exception was "Baby Joe," the canary that he had in his hotel suite.

One of my jobs when I went to his apartment to see him was to open the birdcage and let Baby Joe fly around the suite. He had an assortment of books on how to take care of canary birds. Baby Joe had a bright yellow breast and would perch on Mr. Hill's shoulder. Every time this happened he would smile and his face seemed more relaxed.

There were no children. Mrs. Hill could not have them. Mr. Hill told me in one of our dinner chats that he did not want to adopt a baby because, in Texas, most of them came from a "white trash" background. Of course, no consideration would have been given to an African-American baby. Now, with Mrs. Hill wasting away in Texas, all his attention was on Baby Joe and what would happen to him.

One day when I entered the hotel suite of Mr. Hill, I was pleased to see his smiling face. Baby Joe was perched on his shoulder. Then suddenly a delivery man knocked and opened the door. Baby Joe flew out of the suite and into the hotel hallway. There was quite a scene. Mr. Hill was in tears and almost incapacitated for fear of losing Baby Joe.

With the help of several hotel employees, I was able to coax Baby Joe back into the hotel suite. Mr. Hill was in his usual armchair. Baby Joe flew back to Mr. Hill's shoulder and remained perched on it. I prepared a cup of coffee for Mr. Hill, who sipped it slowly. He was in a state of joy. He was in tears. Baby Joe had returned to him.

The next day I had lunch with Mr. Hill at the Hay Adams Hotel. It was a beautiful day in May with Washington's famous cherry blossoms in full bloom. He knew that I was not enthusiastic about going overseas again. He brought up the subject of my career. I needed to make a decision.

Harvard and the Episcopal Church

The five-month training program along with one year's experience in Ethiopia were great preparation for me to launch myself into my career. There were 18 men that were selected from the program and I maintained contact with most of them.

We first talked about some of the other guys (this was the mid fifties and only men were selected for the program). Then he went to the subject of his wife, Ethel. The central question running through the discussion was; what would he do without her?

He then turned to me and said that he had some counsel to offer. I was startled at first because he said that he wanted to be brutally frank. I was a nice guy, he said, but with degrees from universities that were not in the first rank. And as a result of this, I lacked the "right connections," a major handicap.

I responded by saying that I loved my two alma maters, Duquesne and Catholic University. Mr. Hill said that was obvious, but I should now do things that could make up for my lack of connections with the "right people." He came up with his formula.

I was still in my late twenties: he said, "Take a year off and do post-graduate work at Harvard University." He mentioned the names of the United States Ambassadors who attended Harvard, Yale or Princeton. A year of postdoctoral work, he pointed out, would allow me to add Harvard to my resume.

When the question of financing came up, he said that he

would arrange a grant through his family foundation.

I was overwhelmed with his caring and asked him to give me until the following Monday to consider it. While I did not say anything to him then, I had reservations about going back to a university, since I had just completed seven straight years of studies for the B.A., M.A. and Ph.D. degrees. However, Harvard was a tempting offer.

Mr. Hill attended the Episcopal Church from time to time. St. John's, where he worshiped, is a very charming church on the corner of 16th and H Streets, just a few minutes from his hotel. Following our conversation about Harvard, he invited me to attend church services with him the following Sunday.

Living near the Catholic University of America, I rose early on the Sunday morning and attended Mass at the student chapel. I then went by bus and met him at his hotel.

After saying good morning to Baby Joe, we walked to St. John's Church for the 11 a.m. service.

I enjoyed singing the hymns and the recitation of the twenty-third Psalm. The beauty of this Psalm always moves me. Following the service we crossed the street to the Hay Adams Hotel for Sunday brunch.

Mr. Hill was in a reflective mood. After some conversation about a few of the men who had been with me in the trade and investment program, he pointed out some of the similarities between the Episcopal and the Catholic services.

He listed all the former United States Presidents who attended services at St. John's. Then he said he wanted to tell me what some Americans think about the Catholic Church: "It is controlled by foreigners; is not Democratic and the language, Latin, discourages the participation of people" (This was the 1950s). His critical remarks about my church shocked me and evidently I showed it in my face. He observed that the

Episcopal service was very similar to the Catholic Mass. If I became an Episcopalian, I would have all sorts of excellent contacts.

I had a few seconds to make a judgment call. I decided I did not want to be upset with him as I felt deeply that he was thinking about my best interest. I decided to tell him a little about my parents and grandparents—Irish and French Canadian. It was more than just religion. "My culture," I said, "is Catholic." I might not always be a perfect member of "the club," but I could not change my religious affiliation.

Mr. Hill stood up and embraced me—in the dining room of the Hay Adams Hotel! I felt a little embarrassed, but it was a genuine Texan response. I knew that he loved me.

It was June and I had already decided to turn down both a Foreign Service assignment in Iraq and Mr. Hill's offer about Harvard. I needed time to inform both my employer and Mr. Hill. I informed the government agency but postponed telling Mr. Hill. I would leave in a week or so for Pittsburgh where I would join the staff of Duquesne University.

Friday was my last day in the office and I had invited Mr. Hill to be my dinner guest. He was retiring from the organization, and would return to Austin to take care of his wife.

We did not discuss the church matter at dinner. But I did bring up the matter of his Harvard offer. He stopped me and said that he knew I was going to Pittsburgh because the University had contacted him about a reference. I felt very bad that he did not hear it first directly from me.

It is always difficult to say goodbye to a dear friend. It was true in this case also. A few days later I was in Pittsburgh starting my new job. He returned to his home in Austin, Texas. Three weeks later he phoned to tell me that his wife, Ethel, had passed away. Then the bad news! Baby Joe flew out of the house through an open window. Baby Joe never returned. His wife was dead. Mr. Hill cried on the phone about how lonely he was.

Several months later, an attorney phoned to tell me that Joe Lafayette Hill had passed away. Since there was no immediate family, the funeral was small and private.

His friendship meant a lot to me; the memory of it still does. I sometimes regret that I did not take up his offer of a year of postgraduate study at Harvard. But I have no regrets about not changing my church affiliation.

Living in Washington, D.C., from time to time I walk by St. John's Church. I have also dropped in, as I love the tranquility of the historic church. In my mind I think about numerous Presidents who have worshiped there. It is a beautiful building in the heart of our nation's capital a few hundred feet from the White House. I have since then been there on several occasions for services. When I am near the church I sometimes flash back to Mr. Hill, the friendly, gregarious, overweight Texan. He had a formula for success that was appropriate for him and for others. Material success, however, did not spare him from many lonely years, especially at the end of his passage on earth.

I did not accept his formula for success, but I still love the memory of the man.

CHAPTER VI

MARGARET, AFRICAN AFFAIRS, AND EXCITING TIMES

THE BEGINNING OF THE 1960s WAS AN IMPORTANT PERIOD IN MY LIFE. I MET and married Margaret and I had a full decade of experience working in African affairs. From 1956 to 1959 I served as Director of Public Relations and Development at Duquesne University.

While my assignment in Pittsburgh at Duquesne was interesting, it was not totally rewarding, as I thought frequently of my experiences in Ethiopia and my studies in African affairs. The Ethiopian experience left an imprint on me that never disappeared in the sunset of passing time.

The slightly more than one year in Africa, in 1955-1956, was like a *Tale of Two Cities*. One was the knowledge of the immense opportunity for the African peoples who in the 1950s were at the eve of the long-awaited period of independence. The other was the obvious enormity of the challenge facing them from the unholy trinity of poverty, illiteracy, and disease.

I was an optimist: I believed that determination, good will, and competence could turn around the situation in Black Africa. The determination lasted through the 1960s. It was to focus into a more realistic feeling later. A new opportunity was given to me.

The opportunity in New York City had three aspects to it; two provided assurance of income. The first one was on the staff of John Price Jones, a fund-raising firm. Charles Anger, the president of the firm, offered me a job at the level of three-quarter time. St. John's University was initiating a major in African affairs and offered me the appointment of a visiting professorship, teaching one course on Saturday mornings.

The third opportunity was less definite as far as compensation was concerned. Father John LaFarge, the Jesuit activist, and Rawson L. Wood, an active Catholic layman in the civil rights movement, had developed plans for an organization that would assist African students at U. S. colleges and universities.

This third project was for me the most exciting aspect of my going to New York City. In the spring of 1959 I said goodbye to my friends and associates at Duquesne University and drove to New York City. It was a thrilling moment for me. I would be in the big city, close to the United Nations, where so many African issues were on the front burner of discussion and action.

Youth Service Abroad: The Peace Corps

In 1960, following the publication of my Profiles of African

Faith—Family—Friends 63

Leaders, I had many speaking engagements. In these talks, I developed the concept of American Youth serving as volunteers overseas. I was invited to speak at the Princeton University conference on youth service, November 11-12, 1960.

My plan would have had the government assisting private agencies with expenses like travel and health insurance. The volunteers would commit to two years. The local government would be expected to make a nominal contribution to the cost of maintaining the volunteers.

My visits to the campuses convinced me that there was a tremendous source of good will and energy among American students and that this would be utilized for overseas volunteer service like teaching.

Toward the end of the 1960 presidential campaign, Senator John Kennedy proposed a "Peace Corps" of American youth to assist the developing countries. His plan called for the creation of a government agency.

I had sent my proposal to Vice President Nixon, but was told that the proposal was risky. *The New York Times* in a November 10, 1960 article on the various plans for overseas service described me as "an originator of the Peace Corps project."

There were clear differences in the proposals. Mine would have utilized private agencies, while the Kennedy plan was for a new governmental agency.

Despite my being the early author of proposals for youth service abroad, I was not invited by the Kennedy administration to assist in the planning for the government program.

Several years later, while attending the dinner of President Johnson for Emperor Haile Selassie of Ethiopia, Sargent Shriver, Peace Corps Director (and brother-in-law of John F. Kennedy) referred to my "authorship" of youth service proposals.

Friends urged me later, on the tenth and twentieth anniversary celebrations of the Peace Corps, to set out my claim as an originator of the proposal. I was reluctant to do this.

Three Jobs

By the fall of 1960, eighteen months after my arrival in New York, I was having a tough time juggling three jobs. Fortunately, the African project grew, and by early 1960, African Service Institute was founded. It functioned until 1961 as a division of the Catholic Inter-racial Council of New York.

As soon as the U.S. government granted A.S.I. tax-exempt status, it became independent of the Council. The A.S.I.'s charter established three main goals:

1. Obtain scholarships for African students at U.S. colleges and universities, and assist these students in obtaining summer employment;

2. Assist African families with finding housing in New York;

3. Provide the struggling African states with refugee assistance.

A new board was recruited to serve with Rawson Wood. The new trustees included Judge Samuel Pearce and John Mosler. Monsignor Hanley, publisher of The Long Island Catholic, remained on the board. We soon lost Father LaFarge, as he passed away.

Our modus operandi was to maintain a small permanent staff that would seek resources from the universities for scholarships, summer jobs for the students, and international relief for assisting African governments with the refugees.

The increase in refugees resulted from the situation in Africa. The goal of the Institute was to ameliorate the refugee problem.

The arrival of the Institute in 1960 on the scene to address African needs came at just the right time. We planned that the Institute would be temporary, perhaps ten years. Then we felt that universities would be established in most of Africa and that the new states would be organized to take care of their refugee problems.

A.S.I. grew like a snowball rolling down a hill. Our modest budget provided by the Catholic Interracial Council could not handle all the expenses. The Office of Cultural Affairs of the U.S. Department of State, through the Institute of International Education, assisted us with the summer student employment program.

But we needed assistance so that the salaries of the five staff members could be assured. An offer for help came from government-connected foundations. Before I proceeded with the arrangement I consulted with Church officials in New York City because of our Catholic Church affiliation. First of all, A.S.I. was not an official Church organization; it was very well connected with Catholic leadership. I was told that as long as A.S.I. maintained its independent status, we could accept funds for "good purposes." The foundations consequently were a significant source of administrative support. The salaries of the staff could be assured.

One area where we were able to raise significant resources was in refugee support. By identifying the needs of refugees in Africa, we obtained millions of dollars worth of medicines and clothing for hundreds of thousands of refugees in Africa.

The refugee operation became ecumenical. While Catholic Relief Services remained the major benefactor, Lutheran World

Service, Church World Service, and others also helped.

I myself devoted my time to research and writing. As a political scientist, I was especially interested in the leadership of new states in Africa. My first book, *Profiles of African Leaders*, was well received and I was able to receive contracts for my subsequent books: *Black Man's Future in Black Africa, Faces of Africa, The Revolution of Color, Western Policy in the Third World, Kenneth Kaunda of Zambia,* and others.

I was full of enthusiasm for the future of the African people. I also felt pain, for I knew that the African people suffered at the hands of the European colonial powers.

In my work at A.S.I., I placed a great deal of emphasis on personalization. Through Trustees and friends of the Institute we arranged luncheons, receptions, and dinners. John Mosler and his wife were especially generous with sponsoring these events.

One of my particular interests was to arrange major academic convocations honoring the visiting African leaders so that a leader could give a major address. One of the most moving speeches on the developing societies was given by Kenneth Kaunda of Zambia at Fordham University, where he also received an honorary doctorate of law degree.

During the A.S.I. years Margaret and I were invited to many major functions in Africa. It was a decade of close contact with many African leaders who remained our friends even after we were less active in African work.

The combination of enthusiasm and guilt complex clouded my analysis of challenges in Africa. Only later did I realize that the complex challenges of development could not be answered in one generation. Furthermore, in my enthusiasm, I advocated the Western model of government. I later realized that it was a simplistic solution. The African peoples must find their own way. Outsiders can assist them but only they themselves can determine their destiny. This was later a central theme in my publications on Africa.

Margaret

The most important event in 1961 was my introduction to Margaret. The occasion of our first meeting was caused by my publicist looking for places where there could be a reception for my book, *Profiles of African Leaders*. Joseph Mubiru, a student from Uganda, who was later assassinated by Idi Amin, contacted Margaret Badum, president of the senior class at the College of New Rochelle. Margaret arranged a reception for March 12, 1961. I autographed quite a few books, and also one for her. It is still in our collection: "For Margaret Badum, with best wishes—Tom Melady."

At the end of the reception I asked her for a date for St. Patrick's Day, March 17. We were soon meeting every weekend. By the end of May, I knew that I wanted to marry her. I had turned thirty-four the previous March. She was twenty-one. I knew that the age difference could be a problem. She was very definite. It was not a problem for her. It was in the beginning for her dad, but Margaret was able to reassure him.

There were several amusing incidents during our courtship. She would attend with me various receptions given by African delegations to the United Nations. Margaret was consequently seen with African diplomats, and the rumor spread that she was dating an African diplomat.

By the end of May I met with her parents and they gave

their approval. June 9 was the big day for us in 1961. Margaret graduated from the College of New Rochelle. It was her birthday and she turned twenty-two. Most importantly, we were engaged.

Soon after our engagement, I left for a three-month trip to Africa. Margaret worked at the Africa Service Institute. I saw many of the leaders and worked on my book *Faces of Africa*. I returned from the trip full of admiration for Leopold Senghor of Senegal, Houphouet-Boigny of Ivory Coast, Kenneth Kaunda of Zambia, and Julius Nyerere of Tanzania. I wrote about them all.

We were married December 2 in Bellerose at the Badum's home parish of the Church of St. Gregory. When we returned from a honeymoon cruise in the Caribbean I settled down to the role of husband.

The quiet man who was such an effective Board Chairman was Rawson L. Wood. A very successful business executive, he was the son of a prominent American family. He gave extensive time to the organization and was a hit with all of the African leaders who met with him.

He inspired me in many ways. His work as Chairman was of course not compensated. Furthermore, he never sought honors or recognition.

We were fortunate in the early months of A.S.I. to have recruited a former student from Ghana, Paul Baddoo. His experience as a young student from Africa, who studied in the United States, was of great value. He also knew from personal experience the difficulties that African students had in finding housing accommodations and summer employment.

He established an excellent network for the Institute and served in this capacity for most of the Institute's active years.

In order to increase the family income, I took on the additional job of teaching a course at the Lincoln Center campus of

Fordham University. Our daughters Christina and Monica were born in 1966 and 1968.

While I always focused on African matters while serving as President of A.S.I., I also became increasingly concerned about racial justice in the United States. In 1966, while attending the World Congress of Catholic Laity in Rome, I authored a resolution condemning racism. Later I was able to arrange for a civil rights leader, Whitney Young, to meet Pope Paul VI. He received us warmly and issued a strong supporting statement.

In the summers of 1962 and 1963, Margaret and I visited Africa and spent two to three months there. From 1964 to 1968 I traveled to Africa alone, where I was able to obtain data for my books and articles during these annual summer trips. Margaret used these summers to study languages in France and in Spain.

We had some interesting and amusing experiences. In July 1963 we flew from Bamako, Mali to Conakry, Guinea. The co-pilot on the flight came back to the area where the passengers were seated with a bottle of champagne. We turned down his offer of a drink and watched him consume most of the bottle. He was an American who had fought as a mercenary in the Congo and was working with the small airline that serviced Mali and Guinea.

I had a chapter on Sekou Touré, first president of Guinea, in my book, *Profiles of African Leaders*. When I phoned and asked for an appointment, he said that he would come to the hotel. A few minutes later he arrived with an entourage of police. He invited us to go to his home for a cup of tea. He dramatically picked up Margaret and carried her to the limousine. I followed and minutes later, we sat with President Touré listening to Martin Luther King's famous speech, "I have a dream," during the March on Washington.

Later that evening we relaxed at the hotel, observing that the developing nations offered us new modes of protocol.

I had the opportunity to serve as middleman in avoiding an embarrassment between an African country and the United States. We were visiting in July 1963 our friend, Lady Marian Chesham, in Dar es Salam, the capital of Tanzania. Marian, a U.S.-born English expatriate and confidant of Julius Nyerere said that the president wanted to see me. After some pleasant conversation, he brought up the matter of the Peace Corps in Tanzania.

He said that he learned that the Peace Corps had connections with the C.I.A. I defended the Peace Corps, pointing out that U.S. laws prohibited involvement with intelligence agencies. It was apparent that Julius Nyerere had made up his mind. He said he did not want to publicly embarrass the U.S. government but he did want the Peace Corps to leave. I volunteered to pass on the word to the Ambassador.

Lady Chesham was helpful to me. The Peace Corps did leave and, while there were rumors, there was no official Tanzanian statement that they were asked to leave.

The Institute, with the assistance of Catholic Relief Services, was sending clothes and medicines to Angolan refugee camps in the Congo. In our visit to the Congo in 1963, Holden Roberto arranged for me to be taken into Angola so I could personally see one of the camps of Angolan freedom fighters. Margaret was a little nervous about my excursion into Angola. It was worth the effort and possible danger. I was able to feel the determination of the rebel forces to obtain their independence.

There were two instances where African leaders brought up the question of U.S. Ambassadors. Both Dr. Hasting Banda, President of Malawi, and Julius Nyerere told me during one of my summer visits that they did not want a "colored" person sent to them as U.S. Ambassador.

I tried to understand why black African leaders would not want a black American as the U.S. Ambassador. Dr. Banda would not discuss the issue with me, but Julius Nyerere did. He observed that African-Americans had little or no influence in the U.S. He wanted a U.S. Ambassador who would have some influence at the White House.

Kenneth Kaunda and his wife Betty were always gracious to us. Ken would have us at the official residence for dinner and normally would drive us back to the hotel. He was looking for specialists to assist in building a police and Army force. I suggested that he look at the opportunities in Ireland. I knew that he would find a receptive and friendly reaction as Ireland had fought hard for its independence.

President Kaunda was well received in Ireland. In addition to recruiting personnel, he received an honorary doctorate from the University of Ireland.

As we approached the end of the 1960s, we knew that Africa Service Institute was limited in the years it would exist. Most of the African states had established universities and the pressing need for scholarships in the United States was decreasing. Furthermore, it was apparent to many of us active in this field that bringing young African students between eighteen and nineteen years to undertake undergraduate studies in a totally different culture had some problems. So many of the students did not want to return to their countries, remaining for graduate work. Some married and established families here. The "brain drain" in their homelands was significant.

We were able to solve problems brought about because of racial differences. I recall one that was especially sensitive.

Joseph, the nephew of an African chief of state, was studying for his Master's degree at a university in New York City. He fell in love with a girl of the Jewish faith who came from a modest family background. She was white.

They decided to marry and the African president phoned me. He was upset and said, "I want you to stop the marriage. I did not send Joseph to the United States to obtain his 'L.L.D.,' to marry the landlady's daughter."

Class distinctions existed among the students and their families back in Africa. In this case the couple married and remained happily married.

The 1960s was a turbulent period in Africa. Four friends who were discussed in my books and articles were assassinated. Sylvanus Olympio, President of Togo, Tom Mboya, leader in Kenya, Dr. Eduardo Mondlane, the Mozambique leader and Francois Tombalbaye, President of Chad were all brutally murdered.

I wrote about all of them and stayed in touch until their assassinations. My final act for all four of the friends was to arrange their memorial services.

By the fall of 1968 the Institute was closed. We had our last experiences in the summer for finding summer jobs. Summer employment for Africans was still a problem. One bank executive told me that he could offer two slots for African students but asked me not to recommend those that were "too black."

While Rawson Wood and I were phasing out A.S.I., I was looking into new employment opportunities. Bishop John Dougherty, President of Seton Hall University, offered me a position as Professor and Chairman of the Department of Asian and African Studies at the University. Margaret and I were pleased, as with young daughters, we wanted to get away from New York City apartment living.

We bought a home in Maplewood, New Jersey. Before occupying it in the winter of 1969, there was a major fire and it took several months to rehabilitate it. We actually moved in May 1969. I had started teaching in January and was commuting to South Orange from New York City for my classes.

In July 1969, while attending a conference of Pax Romana in Fribourg, Switzerland, I received a telephone call from the White House. President Nixon wanted to appoint me ambassador to Burundi. Both Cardinal Cooke from New York and Governor Nelson A. Rockefeller had recommended me.

I had been under consideration to be the first U.S. ambassador to Botswana, but the U.S. Senate was reluctant to start an embassy there and so I was switched to Burundi.

At about the time my appointment was under consideration, the South African government declared me to be a prohibited alien. Margaret and I had visited South Africa in 1962. The South African government did not like my criticism of apartheid in my book, *The Revolution of Color*. The ban on my visits was later lifted when the African black majority gained control of the government.

The offer of an appointment was a dilemma. A new job and a new house—what to do? Bishop Dougherty, the university's president, helped me to resolve the problem. He said, "Tom, take it and even though you are not tenured, you can always return to Seton Hall University when your tour is completed."

Margaret and I decided to go to Burundi with our two daughters. We rented the house in Maplewood and left for East Central Africa. Margaret had completed most of her requirements for an M. A. in French Literature. Since there was a university in Bujumbura, she could complete the last remaining course there and work on her dissertation.

I went to Burundi with a certain amount of confidence. By the time I left Burundi three years later, I realized how unprepared I was for the complex task of representing the U.S. in a developing country full of ethnic alienations. I had no idea that less than three years after arriving in Burundi, Margaret, our daughters, and I would be in a country where genocide-like civil strife would take place.

CHAPTER VII

BURUNDI AND UGANDA: THE REALITY OF BRUTALITY

WHEN PRESIDENT NIXON INFORMED ME THAT I WOULD BE APPOINTED AS the U.S. Ambassador to Burundi, I began my preparation by reading copies of the reports by the German explorers who arrived in the mountains of Burundi and neighboring Rwanda in the 1890's. The explorers, who annexed these two countries to German East Africa, wrote in glowing terms about the beauty of the mountains, valleys and lakes of this east central African country. In the reports, Burundi was described as the Switzerland of Africa.

While in Washington preparing for my assignment in the fall of 1969, I learned that in the process of evaluating my credentials that there was a remark at the staff meeting that had negative implications for my alma mater, the Catholic University of America.

There were around a half dozen academic candidates for the diplomatic posts. In the course of the meeting at the White

House, where resumes were being examined, an assistant remarked, "Melady has his Ph.D. in international relations from the Catholic University of America." Another aide said, "I thought that the Catholic University of America was a Sunday school."

Despite that derogatory characterization of the Catholic University, President Nixon appointed me as the U.S. Ambassador to Burundi. Thirty years later while I was serving as U.S. Ambassador in Rome, the person who made the negative remark was my guest at the residence. I was tempted but did not bring up in conversation what he said.

There were two principal tribes in Burundi, Tutsi and Hutu. More appropriately called communities, these two groups had particular characteristics. The Tutsis were generally tall, slim and had a culture based on the migration of their ancestors several hundred years previously from the highlands of Ethiopia. They were the aristocrats and had a feudalistic, or monarchical government. They then constituted around fifteen percent of the population.

The Hutus, around eighty percent of the population, had local roots in the Bantu communities of central Africa. A small community of Twa peoples, (called pygmies by locals and Europeans at that time) constituting around two percent of the population, lived in the countryside isolated from the daily life of the Tutsi and Hutu peoples.

The Germans, like the British and French, practiced indirect rule and thus worked through the Tutsi dominant minority. The German authorities maintained a minimum police force of several hundred men who, according to their reports, "put down" outbreaks of violence between the Tutsi and Hutu peoples. After World War I, the Belgians took over the administration of the Trust territories. They also reported eruptions of violence between the two communities. The Belgian administration, which lasted from 1918 to 1962, produced many reports on the beauty of the countryside. It became a favorite place for Belgian expatriates.

The beautiful countryside was marred by an ugly alienation rooted in almost five hundred years of mistrust. Neither the German nor the Belgian historical records reported the folk tales, preserved from generation to generation, that conveyed the hatred of the two groups for each other.

I also had access to U.S. government documents that did report some of the alienation present in the relationships between the Tutsi and Hutu peoples. Neither the historic German and Belgian reports nor the more recent U.S. government assessments conveyed the fact that the "Switzerland of Africa" image was a benign cover of malignant ethnic-racial hatred.

I had about three months to prepare for my assignment before arriving in Burundi as Ambassador and chief of mission. I was teaching then at Seton Hall University, and Margaret, in addition to being mother to two daughters, was working on her Master's degree in French literature. We had no sense of the deep division that infested Burundi.

We consequently talked about American organizations in Burundi that were in dialogue, working together, implementing the technique of nonviolent negotiations and political pluralism.

I will always remember our arrival at Bujumbura airport. While the pilot of the Sabena airplane circled over the lake, I forgot about some of the concerns that I had from the reports. The arrival plus our falling in love with the countryside inspired me to plunge full speed ahead with the dialogue and "do good" projects that I had planned even before leaving the

U.S. Our first several months in 1970 were spent visiting all the corners of Burundi.

I had talked with my friend, the Reverend James Robinson, founder of Crossroads Africa, and he agreed to personally lead a group of volunteers to Burundi for eight weeks. Jim, an African-American Protestant minister, accepted my invitation to do a project for the Catholic Bishop. It would be a conference center at the seminary for Catholic young men preparing for the priesthood. What an example, I observed, of ecumenical partnership and social harmony—Americans of black and white backgrounds of all religious persuasions working with Black African Catholic seminarians.

I was proud of this project and invited Burundi leaders of both tribal backgrounds to come and see this example of racial harmony and religious pluralism. The Burundi seminarians of Tutsi and Hutu backgrounds witnessed it on a daily basis. Never did I sense that two and a half years later some of these same students would fight one another in ethnic conflict.

I had no difficulty in involving Protestant organizations to assist me in Burundi. In 1971, a whooping cough epidemic struck without warning in the hills of the Northeastern part of the country. It was in many cases fatal to the children who contracted it. Through phone calls to my friends in the Lutheran World Service and Catholic Relief services, I was able to have the life-saving medicine airlifted to Burundi. I was proud to point out the ecumenical diversity in the American assistance. Again, I thought that we were setting a good example in diversity.

We had several visiting Congressional delegations. Since the Democrats had a majority in the U.S. Senate and in the House of Representatives, they controlled the chair positions. Congressman Charles Diggs, an African-American Democrat, was our houseguest when he made an official visit to Bujumbura. We stood side-by-side in the reception line, he a Democrat, I a Republican; he of African descent, I of Caucasian. In both of our remarks we talked about political pluralism.

In my remarks, I also talked about the role of the opposition. I pointed out that the Congressman, a Democrat, represented the opposition at a time when the executive branch was in the hands of a Republican President.

When the reception was over, I said to Margaret that it was a good lesson for the importance of protecting and respecting the opposition. I was disappointed to learn several days later that in the local language of Kirundi the word for "opponent" was "enemy."

When I said that an opponent was to be respected and protected; the translation was "enemy." I was naïve to think that the culture of one country could be transposed on to that of another culture.

In the fall of 1970, I was forced to violate one of my instructions. I had been warned by the U.S. Government officials not to accept any rides in the helicopter of President Micombero if he were to be the pilot. The helicopter had been a gift of France. The French government also assigned a pilot to the staff of the President who had only taken several lessons and did not have a pilot's license.

It was a Sunday and the President and I were attending the late morning Mass at the Cathedral. He rushed over to embrace me after the Mass to say that his wife had a baby boy the preceding day and that the baptism would take place in the afternoon at his hometown village in southern Burundi. He invited me to fly with him in the helicopter.

Without hesitation I said that I would be honored. So I said goodbye to Margaret and went to the airport. While President

Micombero served as the pilot I was relieved to see that the French pilot was there with him.

The trip itself was uneventful as we flew over lake Tanganyika that had plenty of crocodiles!

The mood at the baptism was warm, with the President telling jokes about the number of sons that he wanted. When I left the President embraced me warmly. The "good" relationship was fortunate as three months later I was summoned to the President's office. He gave me the startling news that he was planning to expel the U.S. embassy. "Why, I asked?"

He said that he had a copy of a letter from the CIA to me outlining their plan to fly submarines from Mozambique to the southern part of Lake Tanganyika. The submarines would then advance to the northern part of the lake and invade Bujumbura and overthrow his government.

These documents were forgeries, given to him by the embassy of Czechoslovakia. It was a stressful forty-eight hours. I finally took a chance and pointed out how ridiculous the allegation was, as the United States had no vital interests in Burundi. He then allowed me to bring in a U.S. government specialist on forgeries and he accepted the evidence that the documents were a forgery. He told me that the Czechoslovaks were trying to break up our friendship.

Soon, the inevitable occurred. Three weeks before we were due to leave in order for me to accept a new assignment as Ambassador to Uganda, fighting broke out in the outskirts of Bujumbura on April 29, 1972. The Hutu majority attempted a coup d'état against the Tutsi minority controlled government and killed around ten thousand Tutsis.

The Tutsis entered into a rampage and in a ten-day period, killed over one hundred thousand Hutus. Although it could never be established beyond any shadow of a doubt, there is some indication that the Tutsis had planned this, as all Hutus who had more than an elementary school education were especially high on the execution list.

Our immediate concern was to guarantee the protection of the private American citizens. They, in Burundi, were overwhelmingly Protestant missionaries working with the Hutu peoples. Given the animosity at the time of Tutsi government officials toward any group that gave the appearance of having Hutu sympathies, we feared for them and took immediate steps to inform the Burundi government that we would tolerate no harm to them.

This presented me with a dilemma. I requested and received an appointment to see Colonel Micombero, the Dictator-President. I spoke very strongly about the safety of the Americans living in Burundi. I also told him about the U.S. concern about the brutality of the internal strife.

In the midst of assuring me about the safety of the private Americans, he opened a small, attractive box and said that he wished to confer a high Burundi decoration on me. I had only a few seconds to make a decision. I had some evidence that the government's reprisals greatly exceeded what was necessary in order to end the chaos, and consequently Hutu peoples were unnecessarily being killed. I told Micombero that the massive killing of Hutu people gave the appearance of a genocide.

On the other hand, my primary responsibility was to ensure the safety of the private American citizens. I wanted Micombero to make a commitment to guarantee their safety. In those few seconds—that then seemed like an eternity—I decided to thank Micombero for thinking of me and said that I would *receive* the medal and transmit it to my government, which would decide if I could accept it.

It was a compromise. It helped to guarantee the safety of the Americans and I did not accept an honor from a government that gave the appearance of engaging in a brutal bloodbath. I sent the medal to the archives of the Department of State and never claimed it.

On a sunny day on May 25, 1972, the Dean of the diplomatic corps gave a reception in our honor at the airport. We were departing for my new assignment as Ambassador to Uganda. Killing of local peoples were still taking place on the outskirts of Bujumbura, but the diplomats at the airport were sipping champagne. We tried to smile; we embraced friends and colleagues. But the whole time I was haunted by a question my daughter Tina had asked me two nights previously.

That night she told me that a Burundi classmate of Hutu background told her in her first grade class that her daddy had disappeared. Tina asked me if I knew what happened. I did, but I did not tell her the truth. I did not have the heart to tell Tina that her friend's daddy had been executed.

The Sabena airplane was ready to take off from the Bujumbura airport. Margaret, Christina, Monica and I climbed the stairs. Margaret and I managed to smile and to wave goodbye through our tears. We first circled over the lake Tanganyika; then as the plane flew over the Burundi countryside, the pilot pointed out to me the large freshly dug fields. Thousands of Hutus had been buried there within the last week.

While viewing the field from my window I said a silent prayer and then asked myself: Could I have done more for the Burundi people? My mind went back and forth. Yes, we played a role in protecting the Americans—but could we have done more for the people of Burundi in this tragedy?

I sometimes felt that our preparation for the assignment was inadequate. We were not given any information on the deep-rooted historical alienation. I then made a resolution to write a book, *Burundi: The Tragic Years*, which would tell the world about the cancer of Burundi. I did, but it has had little impact.

Since the tragedy of 1972, genocide has been repeated on two occasions in that region. Thousands in both communities have been brutally killed. Each time I read the reports and think about our time there, I also die a little.

And I wonder: Could I have done more to at least reduce the killing?

Uganda

We had about three weeks in Washington between the Burundi and Uganda assignments. Several days were spent on the Burundi situation.

Assistant Secretary of State David Newsom told me that my record of dealing with the Burundi leader and protecting the Americans there was impressive and a good experience for Uganda.

An American had recently been killed in Uganda and the U.S. government was concerned about the possible involvement of the dictatorship of Idi Amin in the murder. My essential responsibilities in Uganda would be to protect the lives of Americans, to guarantee the landing rights of U.S. airlines and assure that U.S. coffee importers had access to the Ugandan coffee market.

When we left Washington I had no idea that coffee and landing rights would soon fade away and that, instead, my family and I would witness brutality that was more severe and extensive than Burundi. Churchill, visiting East Africa after completion of his university studies, called Uganda the "pearl" of the British Empire. When British explorers arrived in Uganda, they found the Buganda Kingdom and several others. The first black students to attend British universities in the early twentieth century were the sons and nephews of Ugandan royalty.

One of the first universities in Africa was founded in Uganda. Some of its graduates came to the U.S. for further studies. Margaret and I met in the 1960s and we had several Ugandan student friends. We looked forward to seeing our friend Joseph Mubiru. He was waiting for us at the airport on our arrival. He came to the residence with his wife a week later. Several weeks after that he was kidnapped. I learned from members of my staff that he had been killed by the special police of Idi Amin. But there never was a funeral service because his wife could not verify that he was dead!

Expulsion of the Asians

Within a few weeks of our arrival, Idi Amin announced that God had spoken to him and that all Asians (East African name for Indians) should be expelled. In his public address, Amin described the Asians as "brown Jews who were parasites on the local economy" and who were like "blood suckers." He allowed them ninety days to leave the country. They were restricted to taking with them only the goods and clothes that could be packed into their suitcases. In regard to money, they were only allowed to take with them one hundred pounds.

The resulting atmosphere in the Asian community was full of fear: I immediately requested a quota of five thousand immigrant visas but only received one thousand. The Canadian government was more generous and increased their immigrant quota to five thousand for Uganda. We had one very sad experience in the Asian affair: Father Clement Kiggundu, a Ugandan priest, who gave Christina her First Communion, expressed sympathy for the plight of the Asians. Within several days the special police of Idi Amin overturned his car and sprayed it with kerosene. Father Kiggundu was burned alive.

The brutality of Idi Amin was evident in the atmosphere that he generated in the expulsion weeks. His reference to Asians as "blood suckers" and more sensational terms obviously incited local Ugandans against them. Nasty incidents were occurring at the airport. Asian women were having their earrings forcefully removed by Ugandan soldiers.

We did what we could to express our concerns. There was a small community of Goans who had their own Catholic parish. We attended Mass there. Some would chat with us following Mass. We wanted to help. I obtained the one thousand extra visas but we, as diplomats, were greatly limited to what we could do. At least frank talk about these brutalities among the diplomats would place the local spotlight on them.

Margaret worked with the staff and we served lemonade to the long line of Asians that came to the Embassy with their applications for U.S. visas. I would make a point of going outside the Embassy and talking to the Asians while they were in line. The brutality of the Asian expulsion combined with daily acts of brutality toward local Ugandans, influenced me to question the basic principle of having a U.S. Ambassador in Uganda.

Was it necessary to accredit a tyrant with an Ambassador of U.S.? There were many U.S. ambassadors accredited to dictatorship countries. Most countries in 1972 were authoritarian. I felt Idi Amin was the worst. He was as vicious and psychotic as Hitler.

When I discussed this with the Embassy staff, there was little sympathy. Most felt that the U.S. should have an Embassy everywhere and that our presence did not indicate support.

Following the November elections in 1972, I requested and received authority to return to the U.S. for consultations. I raised the issue with the Assistant Secretary of State for African affairs. He thought that Idi Amin would change. He observed that if I could "charm" Idi Amin to be more responsive to our suggestions, it could mean a very good evaluation for me. My several days in Washington were something of a disappointment for me. There was no interest in any of my plans for the U.S. to dramatize its distress with Idi Amin by closing the Embassy or by recalling the Ambassador and having a chargé d'affaires in charge.

"Why do that, it will cost you an ambassadorship?" I heard that comment on several occasions!

Approval of Hitler

The lack of interest in the Department of State in taking significant policy action against Idi Amin to express our displeasure began to change after I returned to Uganda in late November.

The public speech where Idi Amin publicly approved of the way Hitler treated the Jews triggered a White House re-examination of the official U.S. presence in Uganda.

Amin, in a public address, referred to Hitler's treatment of the Jews in an approving way. He said they were killed and buried by the Nazis because they were not good people. I reacted immediately to these obscene remarks by Amin and in a report to Washington urged that the President instruct me to call on Amin and protest his remarks in the strongest terms.

My request was granted. The instructions included the request that I ask Idi Amin if he "meant" what he said. Perhaps he had only read what a speechwriter prepared for him.

After several days my request for a meeting was granted. The command post where Amin was headquartered was heavily guarded. After the amenities I told him that I was calling on him on the instructions of the U.S. government. I said that my government was deeply concerned about his remarks that indicated his approval of Hitler's genocide against the Jews. "Did he really mean it?" I asked.

The thunderbolts followed. "Yes," he said, "the Jews were bad people." Then he asked me, "Mr. Ambassador, how many Jews do you have on your staff?" Needless to say I was startled by the question, even from Idi Amin. My reply, since I was dealing with a chief of State was: "Mr. President, U.S. government regulations do not allow us to reveal the ethnic, religious or racial background of the Americans on the Embassy staff."

Amin then fired his second thunderbolt. He said, "Mr. Ambassador, how many CIA people are at your Embassy? I had a few but replied 'none.'" He then said to me that he could not guarantee the safety of the Jews and CIA at the Embassy. I told him how seriously I took that statement and I would report it to Washington.

Returning immediately to the Embassy, I reported in detail on my meeting with Amin. I was very concerned about the safety of the Jewish members of the staff and instituted a plan to evacuate them from Uganda. There were 18 members of the Embassy and the evacuation plan had to be orchestrated in such a way as not to arouse suspicion. I informed Washington and observed that since it was the Christmas season, I should arrange for the evacuation of the Peace Corps.

Removing the Peace Corps was not too difficult, as the overwhelming number were school teachers and passage for them to Nairobi could be arranged as part of their Christmas vacation: of course once in Nairobi, they would not return.

Over a period of ten days the eighteen Jewish members of the staff were evacuated, one by one. I submitted my plan to the Department of State classified as "Top Secret." Three hours after it was sent, a reporter of the Associated Press phoned me at the residence asking if it was true that because of Idi Amin's anti-Semitic remarks I was evacuating the Jewish members of my staff. Knowing that my phones were tapped by unfriendly intelligence agencies, I responded with a plain, old-fashioned "no."

I learned later that a senior officer at the U.S. Embassy in Nairobi, who thought that my plan to evacuate the American Jews from the Embassy was an overreaction, "leaked" my report to the media. All American Jewish staff members were evacuated safely. One Peace Corps member, however, was caught in crossfire and was killed. All others were evacuated safely.

Amin's anti-semitic remarks continued. I was recalled in February and told that the Department of State was considering the closing of the Embassy as a protest to Idi Amin's remarks and actions. The Peace Corps evacuation had not been completed and we feared that any demonstration of abrupt U.S. withdrawal would trigger an emotional negative reaction against the remaining private Americans residing in Uganda.

They were mostly missionaries.

I left for Washington but Margaret, Christina and Monica remained there. Amin's office was informed that the American Ambassador was going on consultations and would return. For three months Margaret remained in Uganda with the children and I worked on Ugandan problems in Washington. Finally, the White House made the decision that the Ambassador would not return and that the Embassy would be closed.

My counsel on the matter was: the U.S. should not dignify a murdering tyrant who endorsed Hitler's genocide against the Jews. After months of equivocation, my advice was followed.

Return to the U.S.A.

By mid summer 1973, the Embassy was closed. Margaret and I made plans to return to private life. With the closing of the Embassy, there was no longer an ambassadorial spot for me. So after Burundi and Uganda, we returned to university life.

But Idi Amin continued his tyrannical activities. It was difficult to separate ourselves from the ongoing tragedy. After speaking about it before a Jewish group in New York City, I was invited by a publisher to "put into writing" our experiences with Amin. With Margaret as the co-author, I wrote *Idi Amin: Hitler in Africa.*

Following its publication we received threatening phone calls, but we continued our campaign to reveal to the world what Amin was doing to the people of his country. I had many disappointing experiences in the process of telling the story. A principle objection was: what do you expect, he is an African leader and you cannot expect him to live by Western standards.

The evidence gathered for our book was so compelling that I decided to petition President Carter to initiate the process of an indictment against Idi Amin. I urged that he be formally charged with crimes against humanity. Through the efforts of Leonard Schine, a lawyer well connected with the White House, an appointment was made for Margaret and me to see President Carter. We flew to Washington. The morning that we were scheduled to see the President brought a telephone message that the rendezvous was cancelled and that we should take the matter up with Ambassador Andrew Young, U.S. representative to the United Nations.

It took several weeks for the appointment to be arranged. I saw Ambassador Young at his U.N. office. His response to me was clear: the Carter administration would not take any steps to bring an indictment. Only the President of the United States, as chief of state, would have had the power to bring him to trial for his crimes against humanity.

Later Margaret and I documented that the purchase of Ugandan coffee was producing the revenue that financed Amin's brutal special police forces. Again, we turned to the President through Ambassador Young requesting a presidential executive order banning the purchase of all Ugandan goods.

We were again turned down. We then worked with several Congressmen, who introduced legislation to ban the purchase of Ugandan products. The legislation passed, and the revenues going into Amin's police budget were thus stopped.

This economic boycott plus the invasion of Uganda by Tanzanian forces finally brought an end to Amin's brutal reign in Uganda. He went into exile and lives in a small village not far from Mecca in Saudi Arabia.

In both Burundi and Uganda I saw first hand, savage brutality and violence. It made me very determined to seek ways to resolve problems through negotiation, compromise and dialogue. I learned from the Ugandan experience a very valuable lesson. When someone is obviously evil, do not hesitate to call him what he is. The world hesitated with Amin, Hitler and Stalin to classify them for what they were: brutal tyrants. Instead, in the beginning of their tyrannies, the world tried to negotiate. We learned an expensive lesson in all three cases.

Finally, in 2001, a brutal tyrant was indicted for his crimes against humanity. The trial of Slobodan Milosevic, the former Yugoslav leader, established that reigning chiefs of state could be held responsible for crimes against humanity.

The Melady family (September 13, 1957):
seated, mother Rose and father Thomas Sr.;
standing, left to right, Mark, Patricia, Peg and Thomas

Thomas Melady and his bride, née Margaret Badum,
exchange a toast following their marriage on
December 2, 1961

Dr. Melady wearing the decoration "Commander of the National Order of Senegal," which he had just received from Senghor of Senegal (center) on October 5, 1966. At right is Eugene Callender of the Urban League.

Thomas and Margaret Melady with their daughters Christina and Monica and his parents, Mr. and Mrs. T. P. Melady, after taking the oath of office as U.S. ambassador to Uganda, at the Department of State on June 26, 1972.

Ambassador Melady talking with President Micombero of Burundi in July 1970 when the President visited the Ambassador's residence.

Dr. and Mrs. Melady with daughters upon arrival at Entebbe airport on July 25, 1972, being welcomed by officials of Ministry of Foreign Affairs.

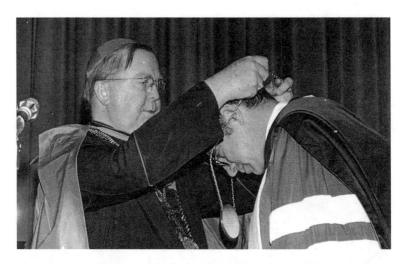

Inauguration of Dr. Melady as third President of Sacred Heart University on December 11, 1976

Secretary of Education Terrell Bell congratulates Tom Melady on his swearing-in as Assistant Secretary of Education, August 4, 1981, while (from left) daughters Christina and Monica, mother Mrs. Thomas Melady, Sr., and Mrs. Melady look on.

Ambassador and Mrs. Thomas Patrick Melady with Pope John Paul II during presentation of credentials in private audience, October 1, 1989

Ambassador and Mrs. Melady with President George Bush, August 9, 1989

CHAPTER VIII

PRESIDENTS NYERERE, NIXON AND THE MARYKNOLL SISTERS

FOURTEEN YEARS AFTER MY FIRST OVERSEAS ASSIGNMENT IN ETHIOPIA, I WAS assigned to the U.S. Mission to the United Nations. One of the great experiences in my African work was my friendship with President Julius Nyerere. He was a noble man.

An African man in a dramatic way distinguished between the important and less important. I was serving as Senior Advisor to the United States Delegation to the United Nations General Assembly in the fall of 1970. At that time, I was actually the U.S. Ambassador to the Republic of Burundi in Central Africa. The Department of State recalled me for the three-month session of the United Nations, as many of the African leaders who would be participating in the silver Jubilee of the United Nations were subjects in my book, *Profiles of African Leaders*. Several were friends.

Margaret, our two daughters and I arrived for the U.N. session in early September. Margaret and I stayed at the San Carlos Hotel during the week. The hotel was a few minutes from the U.S. Mission on the Plaza. Christina and Monica resided with Margaret's parents in Bellrose, Long Island, where we frequently spent the weekends.

It was a very exciting session for me, as I knew many of the African leaders who would be there. Emperor Haile Selassie, Leopold Senghor, Houphouet-Boigny, Julius Nyerere, Amadou Ahidjo and Kenneth Kaunda attended this session. I met them at the airport and then stayed in touch with them while they remained in New York. Many of these leaders were subjects either in my books or in articles. Many of them engaged me in conversation at the airport. I also saw a good number of them for lunch or a drink during the U.N. session.

My primary assignment was to lobby for the United States and engage in fence mending when necessary. The U.S. needed their votes on many issues before the General Assembly.

Appointment with President Nixon

One day in early October, after attending the morning session of the General Assembly for two hours or so, I returned to my office at the U.S. Mission and was told that I had an urgent message to telephone Dr. Henry Kissinger, Assistant to the President at the White House. It was emphasized that it was urgent. I immediately phoned. Dr. Kissinger was in conference with the President and his assistant relayed the message to me.

Dr. Kissinger was outraged that Julius Nyerere, President of Tanzania, would not readjust his calendar in order to see the President of the United States.

The background was this: Before leaving Tanzania, the U.S. Ambassador had arranged for President Nyerere to have an appointment with President Nixon in Washington. It was set for Tuesday of the following week. President Nyerere would fly to Washington for the mid-morning appointment.

The Chancellor of Germany had been scheduled to call on the President Nixon the following day, but he asked that it be switched to Tuesday morning, the time set aside for the President of Tanzania. As a result of the scheduling conflict, Dr. Kissinger decided to switch President Nyerere to Thursday.

Dr. Kissinger phoned President Nyerere and informed him that the appointment was being changed from Tuesday to Thursday in order to accommodate the Chancellor of Germany. A plane would be sent to New York to transport President Nyerere to Washington, where he would receive full honors. While Nyerere was a "problem" to Washington he nonetheless remained very popular among Third World leaders. He was a firm believer in socialism; he advocated and practiced it. His book Ujamaa was at that time required reading at most African universities.

A Previous Appointment

President Nyerere informed Dr. Kissinger that he had a previously arranged appointment for that Thursday and that it could not be changed. Dr. Kissinger asked who the appointment was with? President Nyerere said that before leaving Tanzania he had been in contact with the Maryknoll Sisters who had a mission in Dar es Salam.

The Sisters worked with poor destitute women, teaching

them a trade or craft so they could have the dignity of earning a living. Nyerere accepted their invitation for both a visit to their upper New York State headquarters in Ossining and to have lunch with them. President Nyerere informed Dr. Kissinger that he could not change the appointment that he made to see the Maryknoll Sisters—even for an appointment with the President of the United States.

Kissinger's assistant made it abundantly clear to me that his boss regarded President Nyerere's response as personally insulting. Why would anyone turn down an appointment with the President of the United States? The assistant said it was either a deliberate insult or stupidity.

I was consequently instructed to call on President Nyerere and to inform him of the official concern of the U.S. government. I knew Julius Nyerere on a personal basis. I had nominated him for his first honorary doctorate in the United States at Duquesne University, my undergraduate alma mater.

Appointment with President Nyerere

An appointment was made for me to call on Nyerere the following day. I discussed it with my wife Margaret. We both felt that what Nyerere did was in keeping with his character and reputation. He had made a promise to a group who was helping his people. The Tanzanian leader was acting true to form; loyal to people when they had no power. He also had a natural tendency to help the poor and marginalized. This was true of the sisters. In looking for a way to introduce remarks in a gracious way to an old friend while still conveying the essential message of the U.S. government, I asked Margaret to bring with her a copy of her recent book on Leopold Senghor, the President of Senegal.

It was a refreshing fall morning in New York when we walked to the Waldorf Astoria and went immediately to the suite of President Nyerere. He welcomed us. We talked for ten minutes or so about old friends, including Lady Marion Chesham, a mutual friend then living in Tanzania. We talked about several of his friends and relatives for whom I had arranged scholarships at Fordham University.

Margaret gave him an autographed copy of her book on Senghor. It was then time for me to change the "Tom-Julius" conversation to official business. I said, "Your Excellency, I am here under instructions from my government."

I then relayed the official concern and said that the U.S. government was disappointed that he would not readjust his schedule to visit the President of the United States. It was a dilemma for me as I felt that Julius Nyerere had done the right thing. I also felt that the President's staff could have accommodated Nyerere's schedule by finding another date. This would have been a magnanimous action of a superpower.

Dressed in a sport shirt with an open collar, President Nyerere, smiling and relaxing, immediately said that he had a deep appreciation for the work of Maryknoll Sisters in Tanzania. And then he said simply that he had accepted their invitation to visit the Maryknoll motherhouse on the same day the Dr. Kissinger wanted him to fly to Washington to see the President.

Then he asked me to transmit his regrets to the President and his hope to see him "next time I visit the United States."

Margaret and I then reverted to some small talk about friends in Tanzania and wished him a pleasant stay in the

United States. I believed then and still do that he was a man of high moral principle. On the other hand, as I reflect on it, I can see the value of a meeting with the President of the United States. Perhaps there should have been some bending on both sides.

I immediately returned to the U.S. Mission Office and phoned Dr. Kissinger. He was again in conference with the President and so I talked with an assistant. After telling him about my meeting with Nyerere he replied, "I can't believe it, turning down a meeting with the President of the United States because of a previous appointment with some Maryknoll Sisters."

For a few days I thought that my assignment at the United Nations would be terminated. It was not. Associates in the Department of State later told me that Dr. Kissinger's staff thought I was a "pushover" and did not pressure Nyerere sufficiently to reverse his decision. It is true that I transmitted the disappointment of the U.S. government in a neutral way and engaged in no pressure.

While I officially regretted not being able to influence President Nyerere to change his mind, I felt in my conscience that he made the right judgment. He made a promise to an organization that helped the people of Tanzania. The group had no power but he respected them and he kept his promise. This was a characteristic of Julius Nyerere: loyal to people who have helped his country. Furthermore, he was born into a poor, simple family. Missionaries educated him. Presidents, power and money did not impress him. His decision to see missionary sisters rather than President Nixon was not a surprise to those who knew him.

He stepped down as President of Tanzania and facilitated the orderly transfer of power. Tanzania is today a democratic society. Julius Nyerere retired to his farm and served as a mediator in disputes between African states. He was a noble man who died in 1999. He demonstrated in his Presidency the difference between mediocrity and greatness in leadership.

Kenneth Kaunda: Dirty Faces

While President Nyerere was not interested in changing his calendar to meet with President Nixon, Kenneth Kaunda, President of Zambia, was. As the President of the Organization of African Unity, he wanted to meet with President Nixon. The White House advisers to President Nixon did not want such a meeting to take place. The negative decision was made before he left Zambia for the U.N. General Assembly meeting.

Both as a friend and as a U.S. Ambassador accredited to the U.S. Mission to the U.N., I called on him once he arrived in New York. As the author of *Kenneth Kaunda of Zambia*, I maintained contact with him. He was visibly upset that an appointment with the President could not be arranged. It was reported to me that he implied that there was some racism involved. One reporter claimed that Kaunda said that President Nixon did not want to see his "dirty face." I was convinced that this had absolutely nothing to do with his being turned down for a meeting. It was difficult to convince Ken on this matter.

Both Julius Nyerere and Kenneth Kaunda were fine leaders devoted to the interests of their people. It was a complex time. The African nations emerged into independent statehood at the height of the Cold War between the Soviet Union and the

United States. Cold War politics and power manipulation were normal in dealings with the African states.

In the case of Africa, the race issue was always a shadow over U.S. policy positions as they related to Africa. As time passed and, especially after the end of the Cold War, the African states began to appreciate the significant strides made in freeing the United States from social prejudice.

CHAPTER IX

ST. JOSEPH'S UNIVERSITY AND SACRED HEART UNIVERSITY: DISCOMFORT AND TRANQUILITY

FOLLOWING THE UGANDA EXPERIENCE, I WELCOMED THE OPPORTUNITY TO return to academic life. Fr. Terry Toland, S J., President of St. Joseph's University, was looking for an Executive Vice President and offered me the position. I started my duties there on July 1, 1974.

Since I also wanted to teach, the President submitted my name to the Committee on rank and tenure. Despite some hesitation, the Committee gave me the rank of Professor.

My arrival at St. Joseph University coincided with preparation for its 125th anniversary in 1975 and with the International Eucharistic Congress in Philadelphia. These two activities evolved into two central events for me during my two years in Philadelphia.

First of all, in regard to my position, I knew upon my

arrival that there were inside candidates for the position, but the administration wanted an outsider with a "high profile" background for the position. My published books and diplomatic experience helped to meet these requirements.

I asked the staff to use the title "Dr." when referring to me; not "Ambassador." My colleagues were mostly lay Catholics and around twenty Jesuit priests. One of my first goals was to strengthen the dialogue between the Jesuits and lay faculty. I found that there was too much idle gossip, intrigues and envy, and believed that one way to reduce these negative elements in the community was to recognize they existed and to then set out a plan to minimize them. I had the support of the Jesuit superior and leading lay leaders among the faculty. Graham Lee and Jim Dougherty of the Department of Politics were especially helpful.

In this effort, as well as previous ones, I found that those who were negative about groups working together generally had some internal bitterness, insecurity, or negative experiences that energized bad feelings rather than good ones. Some of the ill feelings were rooted in such minor negative experiences that, once exposed to the light of objective discussion, would fade away.

Philadelphia had a well-defined and established Jewish community. I worked with the leadership of the American Jewish Committee in establishing a Jewish–Catholic forum that facilitated Catholic-Jewish dialogue on issues of common concern. Father Donald Clifford worked with me on this project. My work with Jewish leaders would continue at Sacred Heart University.

These two activities at St. Joe's convinced me about the value of promoting discussion between groups that had troubles in their relationships. There were and always will be those opposed to such activities. I remain committed to their value. Some believe that compromise represents moral weakness, but in many cases it is the civilized thing to do.

Margaret Teaching at the University

Margaret wanted to develop her professional skills. Our first fourteen years of married life had us very much involved in African affairs. After working with me on our book about the expulsion of the Asians that occurred while I was serving as Ambassador to Uganda in 1973, she developed a course on Third World Literature. The head of the M.A. program in education was very pleased with it, and Margaret taught the course in 1975-76.

The course was a valuable addition to the curriculum. I never told Margaret that friends on the faculty told me that there were some sarcastic remarks about my wife's qualifications. She had authored a book on Third World literature, and studied the subject in Africa, but a few wanted to find something negative about the arrangement.

I learned a lesson from this experience: when a spouse or child receives a position connected to an organization where I am serving, make sure that there is total transparency in the arrangements, listing all the person's qualifications. Almost two decades later this was done when I was appointed a Visiting Professor at the American University of Rome where Margaret was President.

A Shadow Over the Eucharistic Congress

Within twenty-four hours of Cardinal Krol, Archbishop of Philadelphia, inviting me to serve as a Co-chairman of the Congress, I knew that there would be some challenges.

Several Jesuits from the community came to me saying, "We do not need an old fashioned Eucharistic Congress that would cost hundreds of thousands of dollars." It was 1975 with the bitterness of the Vietnam War and the growing alienation of the underclass permeating the atmosphere.

My good friend, Father Ed Brady, was also concerned. We decided to make world poverty a major theme of the Congress. Cardinal Krol later invited Mother Teresa, who would be a major speaker.

I suggested that recognition be given to the nations of Eastern Europe that were still suffering from Communist-Soviet domination. The Polish/Lithuanian/Ukranian/Slovak/Croatian-Americans responded with enthusiasm.

President Ford attended the Congress at its closing. The cloud over the idea was abated by the goodwill of a few clerical and lay leaders who selected themes that appealed to contemporary Catholics. Margaret and I were very active in the Congress and saw again some old friends from Africa.

Following the Congress, the Chancellor of the Sovereign Military Order of Malta, who had been representing the Order, gave me the good news that I had been admitted to the Order "in gremio religionis" as a Magistral Knight. I later became active in the philanthropic work of the Order and was raised to the rank of Knight in Obedience at ceremonies in Rome in November, 2001.

Conference on World Hunger

Working with a small grant and the enthusiastic support of Jim Gallagher, Vice President for Public Relations at the University, I organized the World Conference On Hunger. It was devoted to the facts of hunger in the world and to what could be done about it. The Governor and other leaders participated.

An extreme group appeared at the Conference and charged that the event was being financed by "The Vatican and the Rockefellers" so that "they could control the Third World, rich in natural resources." After ten minutes or so of continued interrogations I decided to ask the audience if they approved of my decision to have the several protestors "politely" led from the conference so we could continue with the agenda. The conference roared its approval and I became a momentary hero.

However, I still heard a little backbiting from a few on the faculty. Their essential question was: why was such a showcase event arranged for the campus of St. Joe's?

By this time in my professional career, I realized that I wanted to be with the doers. I liked positive thinking and avoided the cynics.

In the winter of 1976, Father Toland told me that he would be retiring on July 1. The two years of experience were great for me and I would have liked to have stayed for another two years. Friends in the field of higher education had advised me to have four years of top executive experience before seeking a presidency.

But I knew the new president, whoever that would be, would most likely want his own team. I accepted the offer of a few friends who subsequently nominated me for several different presidencies.

I was personally delighted when I was approached by Sacred Heart University in Fairfield, as it was in my home state of Connecticut where my extended family still remained. After two interviews I was offered the position. My personal happiness was conflicted because Christina, then ten and Monica, two years younger, did not want to leave their friends in the nice community of Merion where we lived.

It was serious; they cried about leaving their friends. It made me sad also but I knew that my future at St. Joseph's was not secure and that I should respond affirmatively to the opportunity at Sacred Heart University. Margaret and the girls remained in Merion until Christmas so they could finish the semester there. The burden of selling the house fell on Margaret. I negotiated the purchase of our home in Fairfield.

Margaret's mother, who made her home near us in Merion, also moved to Fairfield. They arrived the day before my formal inauguration as President. I remember their arrival, because Mrs. Badum was very upset about the burden that fell on Margaret's shoulders for the moving of the family to Fairfield. She was right in her criticism. Margaret had full responsibility for the move.

I, however, was not pleased at the time with the reprimand that I took from her, but in the long run I forgot it as I appreciated her love for Margaret and our two daughters. That was more important than an outburst of temper.

In leaving St. Joseph College (it was subsequently designated as a University) after two years, I felt both the pleasure of leaving for something new and the pain of saying goodbye. Despite modern communications which facilitate "keeping in touch," saying goodbye to close friends is like dying a little. I knew that this would probably be a permanent feature of our lives.

Sacred Heart University: A New Challenge

I was very moved by the inaugural ceremonies at the University. In addition to the faculty and students, there were the representatives of other institutions, state and local officials, and my family and friends.

It was a proud moment in my life. My mother and father, sisters and brother were there with their spouses, along with Margaret, our two daughters and Margaret's mother.

A central challenge for me was to communicate the mission of a then thirteen year old University in a state which was overflowing with prestigious academic institutions. I found some aspects of an inferiority complex in the University community, which I immediately started to correct. One well-meaning trustee said to me "remember you are President of a University that is not first class; in fact, it hardly is second class."

I remember that he said that when we were together in a group. That evening I phoned and made an appointment to have lunch with him alone on the following day.

I pointed out to him that our mission was to give people in the greater Bridgeport area the benefit of a university education. The students came mostly from working class families. The university had an open admission policy and we consequently undertook the burden of helping the students to upgrade their skills and knowledge. I told him that I never again wanted to hear the words "second class" in describing the University.

My first few months were spent mostly in meetings with faculty and students. My goal was: to have everyone feel proud of the beautiful mission of the University, which was to give all people a chance for a university education. Most faculty staff responded positively; a few were negative and it was difficult to turn them around.

After six months or so of concentrating on the internal University Community, I began a six-month program of visits to the student-producing areas in Fairfield County. I would always call on the principal of the local high school, the mayor and the local media. I gave away hundreds of my books, autographing each one to the recipient. It was a strenuous effort to "tell the Sacred Heart University" story; to eliminate the image that since it was so young it must be second class. The campaign was successful and the systematic increase in our enrollment started then.

I fell in love with the University within a year of my arrival. It was a great and wonderful ten years.

School Politics

The pace at the University in some ways was slow. I looked for ways to inspire and energize the faculty. I knew these efforts should be collaborative. Here was a real challenge: some had settled in their ways and did not want to change. We had a number of "ABD's" ("all but the doctorate") on the faculty. I looked for ways to encourage those people to earn their doctorates. We offered financial assistance. Several did and we celebrated their accomplishments with a reception and a bonus. We quietly "understood" and said nothing about those who did not grasp the opportunity.

With the increase in student enrollment, I was able to hire more faculty. We were demanding about the doctoral degree requirement. In this way I was able to infuse "new blood" into the faculty. Since we were a "teaching" institution, it was imperative that we had a faculty with new, fresh and invigorating ideas.

While most of the "old timers" on the faculty were tenured, I found that bringing new faculty with advance degrees created an insecurity in some. A change was taking place at the institution and, I soon learned, this generated fear and concern in some people.

I had no easy formula for handling this but to stay in contact with key faculty members to assure them that change and growth would offer new opportunities for all. The first four years went by quickly. In addition to my university duties, my main other activity was in *public* affairs. I was especially active in the Republican Party. Margaret was also active in politics and in 1978 was selected at the State Republican convention as the candidate for State Treasurer. Even though no one on the Republican ticket was elected, Margaret received the highest number of votes on the Republican ticket in Fairfield County.

In 1979, I was approached by James Baker (future Secretary of State), who was organizing the Campaign for George H. W. Bush for the Republican nomination for President. I signed on because I thought that he was a man of integrity and I felt "at home" with his moderate conservative philosophy. Also, his father, U.S. Senator Prescott Bush, had helped me when I was a student at Catholic University of America. I felt indebted to the family.

I was a delegate to the Republican convention in Detroit and supported Bush even though it was apparent that Ronald Reagan would win the presidential nomination. The ticket nominated was a winning combination: Reagan and Bush.

Since I was president of a University, I restricted my campaign assistance to strategy counsel. The Reagan-Bush team won. After being an unsuccessful candidate for secretary of education, I was offered the position of assistant secretary for post secondary-education. President Reagan wanted to eliminate the Department of Education and I was told that the position would last for a year.

It was regarded as a compliment to Sacred Heart University that its president would be selected for the post of a U.S. chief federal officer for higher education. The trustees gave me a leave of absence (without pay) for one year. Margaret stayed in Connecticut with our two daughters and I found an apartment in Washington, D.C. I returned home to Fairfield for the weekends. While I enjoyed the challenge, I had two disappointments.

My boss was Ted Bell, the Secretary of Education. Even though I had been a candidate for the Secretary's position, once he was given the position, I was loyal to him. I was, however, amazed and disappointed at the intrigues that prevailed. One group felt that Ted Bell was too moderate and was constantly trying to overthrow him. Some of the infighting became vicious.

Dr. Anthony Pinciaro was serving as (Acting) President during my leave of absence from Sacred Heart. He was an effective administrator, but without a permanent President on campus, a series of intrigues developed. I could not become involved because I was on "leave." I had always planned to return, as Christina and Monica were still in high school and I did not want to move again until they finished. There were persistent rumors that I would not return. My return after a one-year leave ended the rumors. The University was still growing and I felt re-energized with my return to the campus.

My first priority was to obtain a first class re-accreditation, which we did. This would last for ten years and I thought it would go a long way to clear up the rumors about the standards of Connecticut's youngest university. It helped, but there was the lingering feeling that the University somehow did not or could not measure up to the standards of its Ivy League neighbor in New Haven. It was difficult to sell the principle that the standard for judging a university was how was it carrying out its mission.

Outreach with other Christians and Jews

My experience in African affairs convinced me that prejudice was a serious evil that society should commit itself to eliminate.

Connecticut, the original Yankee state, is also the home home of second, third, and fourth generations of people from many parts of the world. In order to encourage dialogue, understanding, and respect for peoples, I established the Center for Ethnic Studies. People of many backgrounds came together to study their languages, history, and culture.

In the 1960s I met Rabbi Marc H. Tanenbaum, and was always inspired by his efforts to achieve greater understanding among peoples of different faiths, races, and cultural backgrounds. It was a special pleasure for me during my term as President to confer on Marc the Doctor of Laws degree, *honoris causa*.

Experience with Mistreatment of the Marginalized

The University is located on the border of Bridgeport and Fairfield. I had two experiences in Bridgeport that dramatized for me the continuing struggle for dignity by the underclass.

On one occasion when Margaret's mother was taken to the hospital, our arrival at the emergency room coincided with the arrival of a group of ten Puerto Rican people who were escorting a man bleeding profusely.

Around an hour later, as Margaret and I were leaving after her mother was resting comfortably, we were greeted by the head of the hospital who assured us that Mrs. Badum would receive excellent care. While he was saying that, the Puerto Rican group recognized the doctor who had been assigned to the wounded person. They asked, "How is Enrico?" The response was "Oh, he did not make it! I am sorry that no one came down to tell you."

Another time, when I went to the parking lot for my car, I discovered that it had been stolen. I took a taxi to the police station in Bridgeport, where I would report the theft. I joined the long line of mostly minority people. Within a few minutes a senior police officer recognized me, and invited me to his office, where I completed the form about the theft of the car.

Both cases symbolized for me the lack of sensitivity to the underclass. These were not deliberately insensitive acts but ones that show that our pluralistic ideals have not yet, in many cases, been incorporated into the everyday life of our society.

As I approached the tenth year of my tenure at the University, I felt that it was time for new leadership. Should I stay or should I say goodbye? What would my legacy be as the third President of the University?

Bishop Walter Curtis, who founded the University in 1963, had a vision that emphasized the role of lay people at a Catholic university. Since my watch from 1976-1986, Sacred Heart University has flourished under lay leadership. Dr. Anthony Cernera expanded the mission of the university to include residential students.

During my presidency there were programs on Catholic-Jewish issues. The interest in these matters was a good background for the Center for Christian-Jewish Understanding, established by Dr. Anthony Cernera. The center is now flourishing.

It was a perplexing challenge. I felt in my heart that I exhausted all new ideas for the University and that a new person would bring new life and vigor to the institution. On the other hand, I loved the University, and especially the students. What would the future bring?

Bishop Walter Curtis, Chairman of the Board, and other trustees encouraged me to stay. But I felt that the faculty was restless. Perhaps they needed a new leader.

On July 1, 1985, at the end of my ninth year, I announced that I would leave on July 1, 1986, at the end of my tenth year. The university consequently had one year to find and appoint my successor. On June 30, 1986, in a goodbye reception at the University, Margaret and our two daughters presented the University with my portrait. The Chairman of the Executive Committee, Bob Huebner, announced my designation as President Emeritus.

It is always the rumors that are annoying. One faculty member told people that I received one year's salary as a bonus. I neither asked for nor received any such arrangement. It was a great ten years, the University named me President Emeritus for life, and I was able to say goodbye and God bless.

There are many memories of my university presidency. The most precious one is collective impression of the students. I was able to help many in those formative years and quite a few lifelong friendships developed.

As I look back on my Sacred Heart University years I also have a great respect for many of the faculty who committed most of their professional careers to the University.

Both at Saint Joseph's University and at Sacred Heart University, I was disappointed to see a small number of faculty who were not pleased with their chosen profession. Working with young people was for me always an inspiration. I also found it beneficial to be active in local affairs—in the "public square." During my twelve years as university executive I wrote articles on local, national, and international affairs. These would result in radio and TV interviews. My strong belief was always: stay involved. I had little interest in worrying about myself.

Executive responsibilities for senior University officers now require the President to spend considerable time with community leaders, corporate and foundation personnel. It is understandable when the time spent with students is reduced. Various arrangements can assist a very busy University executive to spend some quality time with students. They include a system of internships, attendance at student oriented functions like sports events, debating matches and socials.

I tried to pass this philosophy on to as many of my colleagues as would listen to me. Some followed my advice; others did not. But with most of the faculty I enjoyed the conversations and respected their points of view.

Friends would tell me that I was sometimes criticized for being the eternal optimist. When the cup was half empty, I would prefer to say it was half filled. In working with people I preferred to identify the positive and potential factors in the person. So many of the students I personally counseled are now making positive contributions to society. It's a joy to remain in contact with them.

The spotlight of public attention is frequently on the president, who gets most of the credit when the university does well. The honorary doctorates, governmental decorations and other awards that I received should have been shared with the faculty and staff. I remain in contact with faculty and staff who were close to me, the same with a good number of students. As time passes the personal relationships remain important.

I have returned from time to time to the University. In October 1997, I returned for the funeral Mass of the University Founder, Bishop Walter Curtis. This gentle man who founded the University and who appointed me as the third President was a dear friend. He inspired me with his gentle way of doing great things.

CHAPTER X

MY FOUR HAPPY AND UNFORGETTABLE YEARS AT THE VATICAN

AS I REFLECT ON THE VARIOUS PERIODS IN MY LIFE, THERE IS NO question that my four years, 1989-1993, as the U.S. Ambassador to the Vatican were the most interesting and the most challenging.

While serving in the campaign of George Bush for President in 1988, I advised on all areas, but mainly on Catholic matters. I had known George H.W. Bush for many years. I felt attached to the Bush family because, in the early 1950's when I was a student at the Catholic University of America in Washington, D.C., his father, Senator Prescott Bush, assisted me.

Tell the President What You Want

Following the election of George H.W. Bush in November 1988, I served on the Transition team as an assistant Director. During this time a senior assistant to George Bush said that a Bush administration would not be complete without Tom Melady.

I was pleased with the comment, as I wanted to serve in his administration. What role did I wish to play?

In my heart from the very beginning I thought that I could be of service as the U.S. Ambassador to the Vatican. I had studied the role of the Vatican in world affairs. Margaret and I also loved Rome. I thought: if it worked out for me, what a beautiful assignment!

I saw the President on several occasions during the transition period (Nov. 1988-Jan. 20, 1989) but never mentioned my desire for a specific appointment to him. Chase Untermeyer, his chief assistant for personnel matters, gave me a form to complete, which would be given to the President. The essential question was: in what capacity did I wish to serve in the Bush administration?

Within a day of receiving the form, several senior members of the President's staff told me that there was a list of four to five supporters who had contributed $100,000 or more to the campaign. Two on that list were also longtime friends! They wanted to be Ambassador to the Vatican. The hint was: do not embarrass the President by asking for the Vatican post.

I did not want to be a problem to the President and so I included on the form four positions that I felt qualified for and where I could be of service to the country.

I was home in Fairfield preparing to fly to Washington when I gave a copy of the completed form to Margaret to read.

She said, "Tom, tear it up and indicate on the new one that you would like to be U.S. Ambassador to the Vatican." I did exactly that.

Several days later, Margaret was in the room when I received the call from the President. I hugged her. I am not so sure that I would have received the appointment if I had not been so direct. The President simply said, "Tom, I want you to serve as the Ambassador to the Vatican!" I responded that it would be a "privilege and an honor!"

Preparing for the assignment was a primary task while I waited for clearances and confirmation by the U.S. Senate. My two U.S. Senators from Connecticut, Chris Dodd and Joe Liberman, both Democrats, enthusiastically supported my nomination. Senator Joe Biden of Delaware, also a Democrat, presided at my hearing. There was no opposition and I was confirmed unanimously by both the Senate Committee and later by the full Senate.

As I was preparing for the Vatican assignment, I would meet career Department of State colleagues who remembered me from my assignments to Burundi and Uganda.

The preparation period in Washington in the late spring and early summer of 1989 was full of pleasant contacts with former colleagues. But I was anxious to report for duty in Rome as I felt that destiny had brought me to an interesting time and place in world affairs.

Within a few months of my arrival, I received my first major assignment. The White House wanted to obtain the Pope's evaluation of Mr. Gorbachev after he met with the Pope on November 30, 1989. This was not their first meeting. There had been an evolving relationship starting in 1985 between the Pope and Gorbachev. I had obtained this valuable information from Cardinal Casaroli, then Vatican Secretary of State, several months after I arrived in Rome. The information on the Pope-Gorbachev relationship was essentially not known to the U.S. government until I reported it.

The meeting of the Pope with Gorbachev was significant. In the meeting Pope John Paul II campaigned for "freedom of conscience" legislation, which Gorbachev promised to support. Freedom of religion was a major agenda item. Cardinal Casaroli told me that Gorbachev inspired confidence that he would continue on the path of assuring that freedom of religion would be a fundamental right for everyone in the Soviet Union. Pope John Paul II urged Gorbachev to work toward ending the confrontation between the superpowers.

The core sentence in my instructions from the Department of State was: did the Pope believe that Gorbachev could be trusted?

Only forty-eight hours before Gorbachev and Bush were to meet in Malta, I was briefed on the issues discussed by Gorbachev and the Pope. Cardinal Casaroli also told me that the Pope believed that Gorbachev could be trusted.

I sent all this information so that the President and his advisors would digest it before the meeting with Gorbachev. I learned later that the information was helpful to the President, especially the Vatican opinion on trusting Gorbachev.

The Malta meeting of December 1, 1989 was the start of a two-year Bush-Gorbachev relationship. It was two years later that the Soviet empire collapsed.

Christmas Eve and Noriega

Margaret and I were preparing for Christmas Eve Mass in 1989 at St. Peter's when I was alerted by a phone call from the

Department of State that Manuel Noriega, Dictator of Panama, had obtained refuge in the nunciature (Embassy) of the Vatican in Panama City. I went immediately to the Embassy to obtain my instructions. While waiting for the secretary or his assistant to speak to me I watched the Noriega drama on television. I saw the clips of him entering the Vatican Embassy. While television gave me all the information about General Noriega, the secretary's office gave me my orders. My instructions were clear: The United States government did not want The Holy See to grant asylum in the nunciature to Noriega. There was a great danger that he would become a symbol for left wing elements and anti-American groups throughout the world. This effort to capture Noriega was very important to President Bush. It was the first international operation in his anti-drug crusade.

I was urged to see Cardinal Casaroli that evening, which meant right after midnight Mass. I was told to approach him formally on behalf of the United States government. I declined to do this, as I thought it was inappropriate to request an official meeting at that time. I decided to make it personal. The midnight Mass would end at around two o'clock in the morning. Once I arrived at the midnight Mass, I sent Cardinal Casaroli a brief note indicating to him that if he had a moment I would like to speak to him informally and privately after the Mass. Christmas Eve Mass was important to me. I have never missed midnight Mass. I tried to concentrate on the liturgy, but my mind wandered. I knew how important this matter was to President Bush. It was difficult to focus on the Mass because of my concerns. As I returned to the diplomatic section after receiving Holy Communion, two ambassadors stopped me to inquire about the latest news concerning Noriega.

Cardinal Casaroli approached me after Mass, shook my

hand, and told me he was aware that Noriega had been admitted to the nunciature in Panama. He too had seen it on television. Briefly I gave the Cardinal our position: that Noriega was a criminal and should not be granted asylum. I indicated to Cardinal Casaroli that I would be in contact with him about a meeting on December 27. I knew December 26 was a traditional holiday for Vatican personnel and I did not want to disturb that tradition.

As I was leaving Saint Peter's Basilica, various members of the press came up to me asking for a statement. I was essentially able to avoid them.

It soon became apparent that Noriega did not have many friends in the world. Both at the residence and the Embassy, we began getting calls from people wanting to know why the Vatican was giving shelter to an international criminal. On the December 27, I met with Archbishop Angelo Sodano, substitute secretary for relations with the states, who in fact was the minister of foreign affairs for the Vatican. I informed Archbishop Sodano that our case against Noriega was based on his being an international drug criminal. I pointed out that an indictment had been returned against him in the federal courts of United States many months before. It later turned out that this was a very important fact for the Vatican.

In subsequent discussions with both Archbishop Sodano and Cardinal Casaroli, I sensed they had an appreciation of the essential fairness of the American judicial system. I therefore asked Washington for a full copy of the indictment. It was faxed to me, and I immediately delivered it to the officials at the Vatican. I had made a strong case in Vatican circles for the United States' campaign against drug merchants. We had previously been in contact with Vatican officials on the growing drug menace, and we knew we had their concurrence on the seriousness of the drug problem. Following my meeting with the Pope in October 1989, there had been several strong papal statements on the drug menace.

Along with James Creagan, the Deputy Chief of Mission, I continued to push forward our claim that Noriega was in fact an international criminal. Our sources at the Vatican told us that the drug criminal accusation, as well as Noriega's bad record on human rights, were building support for the U.S. position. American Church leaders contacted me with reports that the Catholic Church leadership in Panama had a very low estimate of Noriega because of his long dictatorial rule that showed a contempt for human rights.

Believing that the Vatican decision would be in our favor, I nonetheless cautioned the Department of State against expecting the Holy See to respond favorably to the U.S. request in a matter of a few days. I advised that the Holy See could not give the impression of caving into U.S. pressure. President Bush's office, Secretary of State Baker, and Undersecretary Robert Kimmitt understood my evaluation, but I received several phone calls daily from lower ranking staff complaining that the Vatican was taking too long. In the meantime, at the nunciature in Panama City, General Noriega was not acting like a grateful houseguest. We received direct reports that he had been cool and unpleasant toward Archbishop Laboa, the nuncio who had taken him in on December 24. Noriega was known for his vehement dislike of religion and had been regarded as the least friendly person toward the Catholic Church in Central America for many years.

On December 28 I presented the American case at some

length to Archbishop Sodano, the de facto foreign minister. Jim Creagan, Deputy Chief of Mission, accompanied me. We reported to Washington that we were confident no permanent asylum would be granted to the Panamanian dictator.

Noriega was essentially given three choices by the nuncio. He could stay, but there was no guarantee that the nuncio would remain at that residence. Once the nuncio moved out, Noriega would no longer have the protection of the papal flag. The second possibility was to surrender to the Panamanian people, and the third choice was to surrender to the United States government. It was immediately apparent that he would not take the risk of being captured by his own people, and so on January 2 he informed the nuncio that he was prepared to surrender to the American authorities providing the following arrangements were made: he asked that a clean uniform be made available to him so that he could surrender in proper attire, and that no photos would be taken of the surrender; he also requested there be safe passage for his wife, children, and mistress to Cuba.

Archbishop Laboa was in contact with United States authorities and was thus able to guarantee all of this. On January 3, 1990, Manuel Noriega surrendered to U.S. authorities. Actually, I saw it first on television. It was only thirty minutes later that I was officially informed by the United States government that Noriega had surrendered.

In addition to the fact that Noriega had been indicted months before the December 1989 incident as an international drug lord, it was apparent from the period of December 24 to January 3 that the worldwide communications community had little respect for him. With the exception of the communist left-wing press, the general editorial comment on Noriega was unfavorable. Certainly in terms of telephone calls—and we had many, both at the residence and the Embassy during this period—the decision had popular approval. All but one raised basic questions about the Holy See's even considering asylum for Noriega. For these few days I defended the decision of the nuncio to give him temporary refuge until a decision on asylum could be made. During this time, I was restricted to Rome; that is, the Department of State requested that I always be there. I would frequently bump into people in restaurants or hotels and there was a great outpouring of support for the U.S. position.

International interest in the Noriega case was an example of the impact of modern communications. Foreign policy decisions were once the prerogative of a few world leaders, and those decisions were frequently made in secret. Now, instant communications bring ongoing developments to millions of people throughout the world. Consequently, international public opinion also influenced world leaders. Academic, church and legal voices can now be raised to influence these decisions. One aspect of the Noriega case surfaced a year later at his trial in Florida. The Department of State informed me that Noriega's defense lawyers would reveal that his telephone conversations from the nunciature in Panama had been bugged. I thought it prudent to inform the Vatican immediately, so they would not be unpleasantly surprised when this was reported in the press. I arranged for my deputy to brief Monsignor Celli. He responded by saying that he was not surprised. There was very little coverage of this disclosure.

The State of Israel and the Holy See: Complex Relationships

The instructions from Secretary Baker concerning Israel were clear and simple. In a brief declarative sentence, he said in his official letter of instructions to me, "You should also urge the

Holy See to recognize the State of Israel." Several months before that, while I was preparing for my confirmation hearings in July 1989, I was told that there might be one or two questions for me. Not knowing what the questions would be, I prepared rather thoroughly for the hearing. At the hearing there was only one important question. Senator Joseph Biden, who presided at the committee hearing for my confirmation, brought up the matter of papal recognition of the State of Israel. He strongly urged me to give priority to influencing the Holy See to establish diplomatic relations with the State of Israel. As other senators in the committee hearing looked on, I had no doubt that he was reflecting the sentiments of the United States Senate.

Consequently I had a double-barreled command: both the Secretary of State, the executive to whom I reported, and the Senate, elected by the American people to represent them, wanted me to focus on obtaining a favorable decision of the Holy See to establish diplomatic relations with the State of Israel. I soon found that the history of the Holy See's relationships with The Holy Land had complicated nuances to it. This was not an easy assignment.

I concentrated on accomplishing this instruction during my tenure as U.S. Ambassador to the Holy See. I had hoped to accomplish it before my departure. While considerable progress was made, I did not succeed in having diplomatic relations between the Holy See and the Senate of Israel established while I was ambassador. I was able to play a role in establishing dialogue between the two parties and to see the official process that would lead to diplomatic relations initiated. But I departed Rome without accomplishing this main goal.

When I left Rome in March of 1993, I looked at the list

of assignments given to me. The assignment of influencing the Holy See to establish diplomatic relations with the State of Israel had only partially been accomplished. I did not realize when I started working on this project that there was a long history of complex relationships involving people, philosophies, religions, and hundreds of years of history. There also were high emotions and some prejudice on both sides. It was my feeling from the very beginning that the Holy See, which I loved and respected, had been ill-advised not to have moved sooner to eliminate the peculiar circumstance of not having diplomatic relations with Israel. The Holy See was one of the few international personalities in the world community in the early 1990's that did not have diplomatic relations with the State of Israel.

Several months after I returned to the U.S. in April 1993, a senior Vatican official confided to me that there would be a solution to the lack of diplomatic relations by the end of the year. In October 1993, when I inquired again, he confirmed that there would be an announcement by the end of 1993. This time I learned that Holy See officials were still concerned about the reappearance of anti-Semitism in various parts of Europe. Formal diplomatic recognition of Israel could enhance the role of the Vatican in fighting new outbreaks of anti-Semitism. The informant said it was being done in the "Roman Way," as it was important that there not be the appearance of caving in to outside pressure. I understood the Holy See's sensitivity to external pressures. I had frequently advised Washington of it and found authorities in both the White House and the Department of State appreciative of this concern.

In mid-December, while my wife and I were in Lithuania, we learned that the goal I had worked for during my assignment in Rome would be realized by the end of the year. On December 30 a phone call informed us that the Holy

See and Israel had established diplomatic links. We thanked God and celebrated with Lithuanian champagne.

The Gulf War: No Convergence

Late in the afternoon on January 16, 1991, I received an urgent cable at the Embassy containing President Bush's response to the Pope's plea that the United States not initiate a war against Saddam Hussein to solve the problem of Iraq's occupation of Kuwait. I was instructed to deliver the letter to the highest Vatican official available that evening. I knew the reason why: the bombing would start the next day, and the United States wanted the Pope to have the President's letter before the bombing started. I followed my instructions. It was a difficult time for me. I knew what my duty was, but I was torn inside about the expansion of the war.

The Vatican Deputy Foreign Minister, Monsignor Claudio Celli, was waiting for me on the steps to the Papal apartments. I knew that war was imminent. My mood was quiet and somber. I believe he also knew that war was going to happen, but under diplomatic courtesies and procedures, we could not discuss it. I gave him the letter from the President, saying it was urgent that he give it immediately to the Holy Father. He said that the Holy Father would have it within a few minutes. I said goodbye. There was not much else that I could say. I left quietly and proceeded immediately to the Saint Damas courtyard, where the car was waiting for me.

As we were winding our way through the ancient streets of the Vatican, I wanted to stop at Saint Anne's church within the Vatican walls. I felt that I needed to be alone for a few moments of prayer and reflection on what was going on, but as we approached the church I decided not to stop there because my bodyguards were right outside the walls waiting for me and they would notice that I entered the church. I was fearful that they would come to the conclusion that the war would start soon. The bodyguards were always with me. That afternoon Antonio, who had been assigned to me since my arrival in Rome, remarked that I seemed "so sad." Many months later he told me that he "knew why."

I therefore told Claudio, my driver, to proceed quickly to the residence. Arriving a few minutes later, I told my wife that war was imminent. I also told her about the circumstances of my visit to the Vatican; I had delivered the response from the President. It was early evening. We had dinner alone. It was really difficult to eat and also difficult to carry on a conversation. It was a long and somber evening. I worked on some papers but accomplished little. Around midnight, I took my first sleeping pill in years. We prayed together that God's will would be done. Several hours later, a telephone call from Washington informed us that the air attack had started.

It had been evident for weeks that the Pope was very uncomfortable with the possibility that there would be an all-out military attack on Iraq. In his letter to the President, which I had transmitted by immediate cable on January 15 after telephoning the contents, the Pope "stressed the tragic consequences which war in that area would have." He went on to say that it was his "firm belief that war is not likely to bring an adequate solution to international problems."

The President's reply came within twenty-four hours. His letter said that "Since Iraq's invasion of Kuwait on August 2, acts of aggression have been visited daily on victims of this war waged by Iraq. The international community has sought relentlessly to reverse this crime and establish a true peace. Our aim is not only peace in the Gulf region but a peaceful world built on the foundations of morality." He went on to say: "The world community stands ready to respond—should I say—demonstrate its willingness to comply in full with the resolution of the UN Security Council."

The Convergences and the Differences

Several days previously, on January 13, at a public prayer service, Pope John Paul II had called for both an Iraqi pullout from Kuwait and the convocation of a peace conference in the Middle East. He wanted independence to be restored to Kuwait but was opposed to the use of military force to accomplish this. The day before, in an address to the entire diplomatic corps, he had unequivocally condemned Iraq's invasion of Kuwait but said recourse to war would represent a "decline" for humanity.

Most of my professional life was dedicated to dialogue, persuasion, and advocacy. I disliked violence with a passion, having seen the worst of it in Burundi and Uganda, where I had served as U.S. Ambassador. And now it was at my doorstep. I knew all the facts of Iraq's cruel invasion and occupation of Kuwait. I prayed that a solution would be found that did not require going to war against Iraq.

But as we approached January 15, I sensed the inevitable. And furthermore, I was an Ambassador, sworn to "defend" U.S. interest as determined by the President.

Several weeks before this, I realized that in all probability the President would initiate the military action authorized by the United Nations. I had studied the just war theories as a student. I knew that it was a disputed subject in Catholic intellectual circles. However, after some research, I cabled the President on January 11 and told him that for some time the "Just War" teaching was part of Catholic doctrine which now has evolved into the "Just Use of Force" doctrine. I said that the Gulf War situation could meet the six criteria of a "Just War" and suggested that the President use this in explaining why force could be justified after January 15. As a former professor of political science, I had discussed with students the criteria for a just war. Relying on that background, my cable said:

Just Cause

Iraq committed aggression against a small neighbor. It was brutalizing the people of Kuwait.

Competent Authority

The competent authority that authorized the use of force was the United Nations. Thanks to modern communications, the debate at the U.N. was witnessed by the people throughout the world—the meetings were not in secret; the issues were publicly discussed.

Just Intent

The just intent, I pointed out, was set forth in the U.N. Resolution: freeing the people of Kuwait and restoring that country to the independent family of nations.

Last Resort

There had been an unprecedented exploration of all peaceful alternatives to accomplish the U.N. goal of obtaining freedom for Kuwait.

Probability of Success

There was every evidence that use of force would be quick and successful.

Proportionality

The use of force and its subsequent cost would be in proportion to the good accomplished.

The Problem: the Fifth and Sixth Criteria

It was the fifth and sixth criteria where the Holy See and the United States differed. There was a clear, overriding fear on the part of the Holy See that the use of the military force to free Kuwait would cause a regional conflict that would match the suffering in the Vietnam War. Furthermore, a senior Holy See official told me that "War is never justified unless every other means to resolve the conflict has been exhausted."

As soon as the hostilities started, my security coverage was greatly expanded. The U.S. and Italian governments were greatly concerned from the first day of our arrival about our security. Margaret and I soon learned to live with it.

The relatively short period of hostilities established that the United States and the United Nations leader had been correct in their assessment that it would be a very brief conflict. But the central fact was that the Pope was not pleased with the use of war to resolve this crisis. Several weeks earlier he had said that "war is an adventure with no return." In the months preceding the January 15 deadline, there were many demonstrations in Italy against the pending UN action. And generally the Pope's anti-war statements were quoted.

On January 12, after his meeting with the diplomatic corps, the Pope came up to me and said he was "thinking of President Bush." He said that he understood "the President had a difficult decision to make but that he was confident that he would make the right decision." I immediately transmitted this message to Washington. There was no doubt in my mind that by the "right decision," the Pope wanted the United States to avoid the use of war.

Not Pacifist at Any Cost

As the Pope spoke against the use of military force to free Kuwait, pacifist and leftist groups took the Pope's comments out of context to use as their rallying cry. I called this to the attention of both Cardinal Sodano and Archbishop Tauran. I was subsequently able to report that on February 17, 1991 the Pope said in a radio broadcast that "we are not pacifist at any cost . . . we desire peace and justice to be instruments of peace. There can be no peace without justice, and justice comes from love and charity." In December 1990, the U.S. was under strong editorial attack in various newspapers and journals in Italy. The two that were most vicious were Sabato (Saturday) and Trenta Giorni (Thirty Days). They were more severe than the communist newspaper. These two publications did have Italian Catholic connections, but when wire services in Europe and the United States reported their editorial comments, they would indicate that the reports were coming from the Vatican. The most violent of the attacks on the United States occurred in Sabato which proclaimed that President Bush should receive the "Nobel Prize for war." I received many expressions of outrage from Americans when it appeared. I took up the matter of these two publications with Vatican officials, who assured me that they were not only not connected with the Vatican, but that actually Vatican authorities had serious reservations about their editorial policies. On the other hand, rather strong criticism of U.S. action in Iraq was also occurring editorially in

Civiltà Cattolica. This is a distinguished Jesuit publication, and it was frequently reported that nothing would appear in the journal if it did not at least carry the silent consent of Vatican officials. It was difficult for me to honestly state to the Department of State that this journal did not reflect, in one way or another, Vatican opinion.

Two unsigned editorials highly critical of the U.S. that appeared in L'Osservatore Romano, the unofficial but yet so very official daily newspaper of the Vatican. These were difficult to explain to Washington. Since I needed to make an evaluation of the articles in Civiltà Cattolica and L'Osservatore Romano, I consulted with my good friend Emanuele Scammaca, Italian Ambassador to the Holy See. I consequently informed Washington that the comments in these two publications frequently reflect Vatican thinking and that in these cases there was most likely a connection between the articles and the Vatican.

Compared to Italy, Catholic editorial comment in the United States was far less negative about the U.S. action in Iraq. This was probably caused by the fact that there was not a united position by the United States Catholic bishops. I was in contact with U.S. Catholic Church leaders during this period. While I knew that my instructions came from the President and the Secretary of State, I also realized that President Bush was in contact with several U.S. Catholic Church leaders. In the weeks leading up to the opening of hostilities in January, the President had talked with Cardinal Bernard Law of Boston and Cardinal John O'Connor of New York. These contacts were his usual ones, as neither he nor the White House staff maintained any regular, significant contacts with the U.S. Catholic Conference.

Cardinal Law was regarded as being sympathetic to the

claim of President Bush that the Gulf war met the just war criteria. He said that prayers for peace are "not fulfilled at the price of granting tyrants and aggressors an opened field to achieve unjust ends." Cardinal O'Connor, on the other hand, seemed more concerned about the dangers of the war.

The strong opposition of the Holy Father to the Gulf War did present something of a dilemma to the U.S. Catholic leadership. But as one Cardinal told me, this was not a matter of faith and morals, and it was possible for a Catholic churchman to differ with the Pope on the Gulf War.

The other two large religious communities in the United States were clear on their approach to the war. The National Council of Churches was strong in opposition and the American Jewish community was generally supportive of President Bush.

The attitudes and opinions of my colleagues in the diplomatic corps accredited to the Holy See varied greatly in those days. The Western European diplomats were sympathetic to our position. My Russian colleague, Jurij Karlov, refrained from any criticism! However my Latin-American colleagues generally joined the Ambassador of Cuba in criticizing the imperialistic action of the United Nations, led by the United States.

The Italian Catholic left was probably the most emotional. Somehow they saw a vast U.S. plot allied with Israel to defeat Islamic independence movements. Because of the extra heavy security protection I had during the Gulf War, I had little opportunity to converse with the average Italians that I would casually meet in the streets of Rome on this matter. But I doubt that they were as strongly opposed to the Gulf War as the Italian Catholic left.

Ground Offensive

The ground offensive started on February 23, and the President announced the cessation of hostilities on February 27. As it became apparent that the war was coming to a quick end, and that those who convinced Holy See officials that the war would last for years and become a quagmire like Vietnam were wrong, there was no change in the Holy See position. In the opinion of the Holy See officials, the decision to go to war in this instance was an error. Their position never changed. They still believe that it was a mistake. It reflects the basic opposition by the Vatican on the use of war.

On March 4 and 5 (1991), a conference on the Middle East took place, called by the Pope. The focus was the postwar situation in the Middle East. Attending were Catholic leaders from the Middle East, heads of the humanitarian agencies, and the head of the United States Conference of Bishops. The Pope called for "peace in the region, interreligious dialogue, and solidarity." He also called for solutions to the problems in Lebanon and Palestine.

The Pope's concern about the overall problems in the Middle East area included, in addition to Lebanon and Israel, the future of the Palestinian people and the lack of religious freedom in Saudi Arabia. The Pope also mentioned the problem of religious freedom in Saudi Arabia when President Bush phoned him on March 8, 1991. I learned that the President was disappointed by his phone conversation with the Pope. He felt that the conversation was "fractured," i.e., ill understood. I felt bad about it, as I had recommended that he telephone the Pope. It was most likely a matter of accent, which the telephone can magnify. When the President phoned the Pope following the Pope's 1992 operation, I cautioned him to restrict the conversation to social amenities.

No Action Against Saddam Hussein

I noticed in the days following the end of the Gulf War that no action was being taken on my recommendation that Saddam Hussein be indicted as an international criminal. On January 18, 1991, I had urged the Department of State, saying, "Saddam Hussein is a tyrannical despot who has committed gross violations against humanity. The precedent established following World War II was that heads and leaders of government who commit crimes against humanity are subject to international law. To maintain this consistency of our actions under international law, Saddam Hussein should be indicted."

I felt strongly about the proposal, as I was the last U.S. Ambassador accredited to Idi Amin in Uganda. I saw the brutality of his regime and recommended the closing of the U.S. Embassy in 1973, as I believed that a practicing brutal tyrant should not be dignified by the presence of a U.S. mission at the ambassadorial level. Following that, my wife, daughters and I returned to the U.S., where I resumed my academic career.

In 1978, after my wife and I obtained all the documentation necessary to indict Amin, I presented it all to the White House and requested an appointment to see President Carter. The request was granted but than canceled the morning the visit was to have taken place. Senior staff of the White House felt that seeking an indictment against Idi Amin was politically inadvisable.

I did not want the same thing to happen to Saddam Hussein but it did. Hussein was never indicted. Various reasons were given: I outlined the whole case for an indictment against Hussein in a cable: it was never answered.

It was these memories that energized me to carry on a private campaign in 1999, to indict Milosevic for his crimes against humanity in the Kosovo War. This time the first step was accomplished: Milosevic was indicted in 2001.

Fortunately the Gulf War came to an end on February 27, 1991. While the U.S. and Vatican differed on this matter, my personal relations with Vatican officials were always fine.

But I knew that I should take some steps to assure the public that the relations between the U.S. and President Bush on one hand, and the Vatican on the other, were okay. I urged President Bush to visit the Pope during his trip to Italy in November of 1991.

This happened in November 1991.

President Bush Visits the Pope

Papal appreciation for the role of the United States in the Middle East peace talks was evident in the meeting of President Bush with the Pope on November 8, 1991. The meeting took on special importance because leftist newspapers and journals, including several Catholic ones, constantly referred to the "coldness" that had developed between the Holy See and President Bush because of their different positions on the use of military force in the Gulf War.

Ambassadors serve as the representatives of their governments. They are also the personal representatives of their chiefs of state to the chief of state of the country where they are accredited. There is the professional desire of an ambassador to be successful in carrying out his or her mission and instructions. Needless to say, a visit of the chief of state is always an important assignment for an ambassador. But for me this was especially important. I knew that the Pope and his senior advisors respected President Bush as a person. They recognized his sound moral qualities as a husband, father, and leader. They felt that he was a reasonable, decent, and courageous man. During the first year of my tenure, I made a point when appropriate to communicate these characteristics of George Bush to the Pope and to senior members of his staff.

My connections with the Bush family went back to my student days at The Catholic University of America in Washington D.C., where the President's father, Prescott S. Bush, Sr., the U.S. Senator from Connecticut, assisted me in obtaining important documents from the Library of Congress for my dissertation. The President's brother, Prescott, Jr., was trustee of the University where I was President. He was also a close friend. I knew and respected his mother. Needless to say, I wanted the meeting to be successful!

This meeting was also important from the public relations point of view. The President met with the Pope alone for over fifty minutes. Only thirty to forty minutes had been scheduled. The President briefed the Holy Father on the recent Madrid conference; his goal for a Middle East settlement; the situation in the ex-Soviet Union; China; religious freedom in Saudi Arabia and Haiti. A good part of the meeting was also devoted to the President's ideas on family, community and moral values.

While the President was with the Pope in the Papal library, James Baker, John Sununu, General Scowscroft and I were with Cardinal Sodano and Archbishop Tauran in another room.

The same issues were being reviewed by our group. While we had no idea how the dialogue between the Pope and the

President was progressing, we knew that our one-hour meeting was very satisfactory.

When the meetings were completed, we joined the President, who immediately remarked to me that the meeting with the Pope was "great." I could tell by his smile that it had been very satisfactory. Since the meeting between the Pope and the President had no other participants, it took several weeks before I learned what the two had discussed. The President told his staff that he was very pleased with the outcome.

The original plan was that we would all say goodbye to the Holy Father. Following that, I was to escort the President and Mrs. Bush and Secretary and Mrs. Baker to a nearby meeting room and present them to a group of Americans working at the Vatican and to the American Seminarians studying in Rome: a total of about three-hundred-fifty people.

As I was about to do this, I was told by a papal assistant that the Holy Father would personally escort the President into the meeting room and guide him around the room to meet the Americans. I knew the implications! By making this unprecedented gesture of escorting the President into the meeting room and presenting him to the Americans, the Pope would clear up the rumors, started by several newspapers and magazines, that there was a "coldness" or hard feelings resulting from the Gulf War.

We were overwhelmed by the way the Pope went out of his way to convey this message. After escorting the President around the room he then praised the President, who of course responded with words of appreciation. As the public meeting ended with the Pope, the President and Mrs. Bush and Secretary and Mrs. Baker saying goodbye, the students from North American College then burst out singing "God Bless America." The President stopped and waved again. I knew by the emotion in his "thank you" that he was pleased with the meeting.

I believe that one reason why the Pope made the unprecedented gesture of escorting the President and Mrs. Bush into the meeting was that he wished in a dramatic way to counteract the vicious images that had been conveyed by several idiosyncratic Catholic publications, especially Sabato. The Pope's personal diplomacy signaled his respect for the President and the United States. There had been divergent positions between the Holy See and the United States on how to free Kuwait from Iraq's occupation. The central reason was objection by the Holy See to the use of war to free Kuwait.

After some time passed and President George H.W. Bush retired from active public life, Vatican officials told me that their respect for him grew. In my opinion it was very simple: President Bush was a gentleman.

Personal Experience

In my work as Ambassador I focused on the matters of state between the United States and the Vatican. I avoided all attempts to involve myself in any discussions that would indicate my preference for one member of the hierarchy over the other. The one area that I discreetly investigated was the procedure for Catholics to obtain an annulment of their marriage.

One of my closest friends at age forty-five had a distressing experience of his wife leaving him with three children for another man. After several lonely years he received a civil divorce, met a woman, and married her in a civil ceremony. He would visit me and we would attend Mass together but he, obedient to a strict interpretation of the rules, would not receive Communion.

On one occasion, I urged him to consult the marriage tribunal in his diocese. The tribunal discovered that his first wife had no understanding of the permanency of commitment. My friend was granted an annulment. I will always remember when we attended Mass together the Sunday after he received the annulment. He quietly wept, when, after eleven years, he received Communion.

Some Catholic visitors would confide in me about their second marriage, which was in a civil ceremony. There was nothing that I could do officially, but I would encourage them to seek consultation with the tribunal to determine if grounds existed for making a petition for granting an annulment. I would hear from some of them who proceeded with my advice. While all requests were not granted, the petitioners were treated with respect and courtesy.

I was pleased to note as an American Catholic that the Church in the United States had developed the structures to determine if there are grounds for an annulment. Unfortunately, the process for determining if there are grounds for an annulment is still not fully established in some Eastern European and African countries.

Time to say goodbye

I knew that saying goodbye to our colleagues and friends in Rome and at the Vatican would not be easy.

Our departure date was set for March 1, 1993. We would leave by the night train to Munich where we would begin a three-week tour—visiting friends that included a stop in

Sweden to buy a Saab and concluded with visiting Tina and her family in Paris.

On our last Sunday afternoon in Rome, Margaret and I made our farewell visit to Saint Peter's Basilica in Vatican City. In the excavations beneath the magnificent main altar, we knelt at the Tomb of Saint Peter and prayed that God would continue to inspire Pope John Paul II in his campaign for human rights and religious freedom. Leaving the crypt below, we stopped at Michelangelo's Pieta and were overwhelmed, as always, by the beauty of this masterpiece.

Since the official car was waiting for us at the rear of the Basilica, we passed in front of the Swiss guards. I took my last salute from them as the U.S. Ambassador. Our car then proceeded over the Tiber river and east to the Trevi Fountain, where we joined the laughing, joyous Romans and tourists. It was Roman sunset time. We each threw coins into the fountain and whispered our wish—to return one day to Rome. The following day, Monday, passed quickly with farewell calls. Finally it was Monday night, March 1, 1993, around 7:30 in the evening. Margaret and I were at Termini, the railway station in Rome, where we had been many times, but this was to be our last visit for some time. We had been accompanied to the train station by my immediate staff: Cameron Hume, Damian Leader, and Ted Osius. Also with us were my two drivers, Umberto and Claudio, the police escorts, and my two bodyguards, Pietro and Franco.

We chatted in pleasant banter on the train platform about our many memorable experiences in Rome. Suddenly we knew we had to say goodbye. It was difficult to hold back the tears, as we had loved Rome and everyone knew it. Finally, Cameron said lightly, "We'll be seeing you," as Margaret and I, along with Pietro and Franco, boarded the night train for

Munich. We went to our compartment, inviting Pietro and Franco in to have a drink with us. We chatted some more about a few of the interesting things we had done during our stay in Rome, than embraced and said goodbye. The two bodyguards would actually accompany us all the way to the Italian-Swiss border. As the train pulled out of the station, we kept on smiling and waving. The tears came later. Margaret and I had a few more glasses of champagne. We thanked God for the opportunity to serve at the Vatican and slept until we were awakened by the porter in Munich.

We then began to focus on the future and what it would bring!

CHAPTER XI

THE LAST GOODBYE: ONLY 10 MINUTES

My friendship with Heinz had two emotional high points to it: several months after we first met in 1950 as university students and the second one in 1999 when I visited him in Bonn.

In 1950 Heinz was one out of the first exchange students to come to the United States from Germany after World War II. I was in the first year of graduate studies at the Catholic University of America in Washington, D.C. and I was living in Graduate Hall.

A week or so after I moved into the dormitory, the Dean of Men called me to his office and informed me that four students from Germany and Austria would be living in the same dormitory. They were part of a larger contingent of German students coming to the United States. It was the first such group of German students to come to the United States after World War II.

Most of the guys in the dorm were World War II veterans;

some after four or five years of combat in Europe; others, like myself, were veterans of the post-war peacetime Army.

The Dean wanted to make sure that there was a good spirit in the dorm and on campus toward the German and Austrian students. I remarked that I had already met them, and that they seemed friendly and the initial response by the American students had been favorable.

The first few weeks were full of all the fun and excitement of starting classes, new friends and the general joyous atmosphere of the campus. Friday and Saturday were the big social nights. In my era, Friday was one with the guys and Saturday was date night.

At the Catholic University of America the overwhelming number of students were Catholic and so on Sunday it was Mass in the morning, a leisurely afternoon, and preparation for Monday classes on Sunday evening.

There were lots of bull sessions, especially at our meals. Heinz and I frequently sat at the same table. I thought it prudent not to bring up topics related to the war. All seemed to be going well and the German boys participated actively in all other social activities, including dating the American girls on campus. They also played on our softball team.

The Dean asked me several times how things were going with the German-American mix on campus. It all seemed to be going well and that was my evaluation to him.

Mid-October 1950

In October 1950 an incident occurred that exposed my "no problem" comment as superficial and premature. It was a long weekend in October. The favorite bar in Brookland, the local neighborhood of the university, was packed. It gave every indication of being a great night for the boys!

Around 11:30 p.m.—after many of the guys had too many drinks—Jack, a law student and a four-year veteran of the war in Europe, started an argument with George, one of the German students. A fight broke out. Others were involved. Terms like "G.D. Nazi" punctuated the air. Heinz, who was seated next to me, rushed over to assist his German buddy.

The tension and fighting grew and the bartender called in the local police. By the same time the police arrived, calmer heads prevailed. The fighting had stopped. Heinz and I said, "let's call it quits and go back to the dorm." We convinced the police that there would not be a recurrence and that we would return to the dorm and be "good boys." The police issued no arrest warrants. The Catholic University connection helped.

Needless to say, that Friday night event was a source of conversation on campus. Some were interested in putting blame on one party or the other. There were those who felt that it was too soon to bring German veterans to the United States as students living in the same dorm with American veterans.

Heinz and I felt differently. We were students at a Catholic University. Certainly here the major emphasis should be on reconciliation. It was not easy. I was surprised at the number of students who talked about the responsibility of "all Germans" for the outrageous conduct of the Nazis. For me this was the doctrine of collective guilt and contrary to basic Judeo-Christian teachings.

The prevailing feeling was more pragmatic: "The war is over, let's forget about it." After that, there were fewer discussions in the dorm dining room about the war.

Several years later Heinz and I both completed our graduate studies. He immediately returned to Germany and I started my first job in Washington, D.C. We maintained contact with each other. I visited him in Germany several times. We sometimes commented on the Friday night brawl and the implications of it. Both of us became involved in interreligious dialogue and efforts at reconciliation in our respective countries.

Final Goodbye

In 1999, I was in Bonn for a few days. I phoned Heinz in advance and he invited me to join him for dinner. I met him the evening of my arrival. He selected a small restaurant with a table in the corner next to a window where we leisurely reminisced about many things.

I was shocked when I looked at him, pale and with a cane. After a warm embrace we sat down; he, as he did forty-six years previously, drank beer. My tastes had changed to wine. By the time the evening was over, he consumed quite a few mugs of beer; I liquidated a bottle of my favorite Riesling wine. The bias and bitterness that Heinz and I witnessed on the campus in the early 1950's was still around. He commented on the situation in Germany and Europe; I in the United States. The biases were now aimed at different targets: hate and intense dislikes could burst out at any time and place. But sensible and cool leadership could end such outbursts before they became bloody.

On the plus side, we commented that there was a full reconciliation between Americans and Germans. We both witnessed a great improvement in the relations between Jews and Christians. We favorably commented on the role of Pope John Paul II in bringing this about.

Heinz felt that the new challenge in Germany was with the prevailing attitudes toward the immigrants. I observed that the world of modern technology was exacerbating the differences in the United States between the underclass and the "best and the brightest." I also had the experience of a genocide taking place in Burundi when I was the Ambassador and a blood bath directed by Idi Amin in Uganda during my tenure as a U.S. Ambassador there. I told Heinz that I felt one reason for the lack of a continuous Western effort to end discrimination and suffering in Africa was that these countries were less important to the West. When such incidents occur in Europe the world, especially the U.S., is more likely to respond.

We talked about the improvements and about the problems that still remained. Without realizing it we were approaching the time to say goodbye. It was a great evening talking about the old days. It was around 1:30 a.m., the same approximate time, forty-six years previously, when Heinz and I helped to break up a fight between American and German Veterans at a bar in the Brookland section of Washington, D.C.

Heinz said to me, "Tom, I have asked my son to pick me up. I cannot drive. He will be here in ten minutes. I have something to tell you."

"We are both getting older," he said. "You look fine but I am not so well." In brief, declarative sentences he told me the stark truth about his spreading cancer that was complicated by diabetes. He also told me that the doctors believed he only had a few months to live.

I was overwhelmed. This would be the final goodbye and we had only ten minutes to talk. We recalled a previous visit in Munich when our wives were with us.

After an evening of celebrating in a pub in Munich we rushed to the train station. As the train was pulling out of the station, Margaret and I, with the help of Heinz, were pulling our suitcases along with us. And then Heinz sang

"Aufwiedersehen." There were other good times in Rome, Frankfurt and Washington.

At that point the ten minutes of our final goodbye was up. His son arrived. Heinz said, "Thank God for the memories." We embraced. His son and I assisted him into the car. The son then embraced me and thanked me for my friendship with his dad. We waved at each other and the car sped away.

The ten minutes that we had after he told me that it would be the final goodbye are characteristic of modern life. We are so rushed that we have little or no time to say hello and goodbye.

I hailed a taxi for the return trip to my hotel. It was late, I was tired and normally a bottle of wine is sufficient to quickly put me to sleep. But that night I tossed and turned. The memories came back of the love-pain experiences of only a few minutes for the final goodbye.

CHAPTER XII

MEMORIES OF BLUEBERRIES AND A KISS ON THE LIPS

EXPERIENCES WITH MY MOTHER TAUGHT ME TO BE ATTENTIVE ABOUT THE future of programs for senior citizens. I was with my two sisters, Peg and Pat, when my mother breathed her last at a nursing home on May 6, 2000 in Madison, Connecticut. She was almost ninety-four.

My mother had global dementia for the last three years and normally did not know who I was. I always had a mixture of feelings when I visited her at the nursing home. And I would always recall Norwich, my boyhood home, on my visits. There she took very good care of her four children and assisted our father at a mom-and-pop package store.

My father was a first generation Irish-American and my mother was a first generation French-Canadian. Mother, to the chagrin of our Irish relations, practiced the French-Canadian custom of kissing close relations on the lips. Kissing on the cheek was reserved for friends. The cold handshake was for business deals.

Time had been basically good to my mother. After the passing of my father in 1979, my mother remained in the family home for five years.

She then made the transition to a retirement home, and to assisted living and finally to a nursing home. There she was struck with dementia at age ninety. Although she lost ninety to ninety-five percent of her memory, she did not have the pain associated with other ailments and diseases.

In my visits to Madison, she would talk about the weather and the flower garden outside her room, but she did not recognize me. One spring, our daughter Christina came from Paris with her then nine-month old daughter, Alexander, for a visit. Mother kissed the baby on the lips, as she always did with babies, but she did not know that the baby was her great-granddaughter. Christina and I shed a few tears, but we were thankful that she was free from pain and suffering.

Every time I went to see her in Madison, I had flashes of our family life in Norwich. My picturesque hometown of around thirty-two thousand in eastern Connecticut was where my mother spent almost all of her adult life. We lived in the working-class section on the East Side of Norwich.

Mother worked in the family store afternoons and on Saturdays. Because the store sold liquor, we four kids could not help relieve my father from his long workday of 9 a.m. to 9 p.m. six days a week until we were twenty-one. And then we were away for university studies.

In those days, Mom took care of our grandfather and two uncles. All three in the end were bedridden, but she was there serving them with loving care.

Her children could not do that. All four of us, and our spouses, worked. Our solution was to find a "home away from home" that could take good care of her. We depended on the safety network that has been set up for our senior citizens. All civilized societies and decent people take care of their senior citizens. My brother Mark and his wife Barbara considered fixing up their home so that Mom could be accommodated, but we were told that she needed the twenty-four hour care of a nursing home.

I will never forget one visit around her 91st birthday. It was a comfortably warm day around three o'clock in the afternoon. My mother greeted my wife and me by asking us who we were. She had no memory of us. It was snack time at the home and we wheeled her into the reception room, where we all had a chocolate sundae. She opened the several packages of presents that we brought, admiring especially the bright colors of a blouse.

Suddenly, she turned to me and called me by my boyhood name. "Tommy," she said, "do you still love blueberries?" That was one of my favorite foods and we frequently had them on Sunday.

I embraced her and she kissed me on the lips as she used to. We both had tears in our eyes. But it was a fleeting moment.

Twenty minutes later, we were back in her room and she was telling me—a stranger to her—that she liked the beautiful colors on her new bedspread.

Then it came time to leave. She kissed my wife and me on the cheeks. The French-Canadian greeting for friends, not for saying goodbye to family.

I went back many times to see her in Madison and kissed her on the lips, but she never again called me by my boyhood name. Neither did she ever again ask about my boyhood addiction to blueberries.

I actually had another occasion where I could kiss my mother. It was her last thirty minutes on earth. My sisters Peg and Pat were with her at her death bed: my mother loved music boxes; her favorite one was next to her bed. I turned it on for the final, quiet serenade. I kissed her lightly on the lips as the tears streamed down my cheeks.

And as she closed her eyes I said goodbye.